Jim Haynes was born in Sydney, attended Sydney Boys' High School and Sydney Teachers' College and then went bush to teach in towns like Menindee, on the Darling River, and Inverell in northern New South Wales. In between stints 'in the bush' he spent several years working in Britain and also gained two master's degrees in literature, from the University of New England and the University of Wales.

Throughout his teaching career, Jim was usually in a band or group as a singer. He started the Bandy Bill & Co Bush Band in 1977 and also worked in radio on 2NZ Inverell and the ABC's popular *Australia All Over* program.

A major career change in 1988 saw him signed as a solo recording artist to Festival Records. Other record deals followed, along with hits like 'Mow Ya Lawn', 'Since Cheryl Went Feral' and 'Don't Call Wagga Wagga Wagga'.

Jim has written and compiled over twenty books and released many albums of his own songs, verse and humour. He still works as an entertainer and has a weekend Australiana segment on Radio 2UE's long-running *George and Paul* show.

Jim lives at Moore Park in Sydney with his wife, Robyn.

ALSO BY JIM HAYNES

Australia's Best Unknown Stories

The Best Australian Yarns

The Best Australian Bush Stories

The Best Australian Sea Stories

The Best Australian Trucking Stories

Best Australian Racing Stories

The Big Book of Verse for Aussie Kids (editor)

THE BEST GALLIPOLI YARNS AND FORGOTTEN STORIES

JIM HAYNES

ALLEN&UNWIN
SYDNEY · MELBOURNE · AUCKLAND · LONDON

First published in 2015

Copyright © Jim Haynes 2015

All rights reserved. No part of this book may be reproduced or transmitted in
any form or by any means, electronic or mechanical, including photocopying,
recording or by any information storage and retrieval system, without prior
permission in writing from the publisher. The Australian *Copyright Act 1968*
(the Act) allows a maximum of one chapter or 10 per cent of this book, whichever
is the greater, to be photocopied by any educational institution for its educational
purposes provided that the educational institution (or body that administers it) has
given a remuneration notice to the Copyright Agency (Australia) under the Act.

Allen & Unwin
83 Alexander Street
Crows Nest NSW 2065
Australia
Phone: (61 2) 8425 0100
Email: info@allenandunwin.com
Web: www.allenandunwin.com

Cataloguing-in-Publication details are available
from the National Library of Australia
www.trove.nla.gov.au

ISBN 978 1 76011 179 3

Set in 12/15 pt Minion Pro by Midland Typesetters, Australia
Printed and bound in China by Hang Tai Printing Company Limited

10 9 8 7 6 5 4

This book is for Angus, Brigid, Ella, Emma-Kate, Fionn, Marcus, Niamh, Penelope, Rhiannon, Samuel and Veronica . . .

Lest We Forget.

CONTENTS

PREFACE

This book is a collection of stories and verse, which tell the 'story' of the Gallipoli campaign, with the events in chronological order, for the layman, or any Australian who has ever wondered what happened at Gallipoli, what it was like and why it is so important to all Aussies.

Included are some first-hand accounts of the experiences of the Anzacs at Gallipoli. Some of them were written soon after the events they describe, while others were written later, in hindsight. All of these accounts were written as 'stories' rather than diaries or military reports.

Other stories and verses chronicle the impact of the conflict on those waiting at home and the reactions of writers and journalists to the whole affair once they had met with, and spoken to, the survivors of the campaign.

This collection is *not* an attempt to give the military history of the Gallipoli campaign or to analyse it tactically. There is, however, a brief background to the campaign, which hopefully puts it into historical and geographical context.

The bulk of the stories and accounts of the campaign collected together here have long been unavailable to the general reader. Some have never been published before and some have been out of print since the 1920s.

I have arranged the writings in chronological order to produce what I feel is a coherent and readable collection. I tried to collect together varied and disparate stories and verses that convey the feelings and emotional impact of the campaign, and help us to understand why the whole Anzac experience has become so iconic and special in our Australian culture.

The first section deals with enlistment and reactions to the news of the outbreak of war. The second section deals with the actual invasion of the peninsula and events on 25 April 1915, and the third with the repercussions of the invasion.

The Ottoman counter-attacks in May have a section of their own, as do the truce, and the Allied offensive of August.

There is a section containing observations and reflections on the campaign and everyday life at Anzac, and another which covers the winter stalemate and evacuation. The final section contains stories and accounts dealing with the aftermath of the whole experience, both at the time and up to the present.

Feelings of nationhood and self-sacrifice abound in these stories and the essential thematic element is the unique Aussie character and attitude displayed in the stoic, incredibly brave and good-humoured actions and attitudes of these amazing men.

Jim Haynes
April 2015

THE TWENTY-FIFTH OF APRIL

RODERIC QUINN

Written at the end of World War I

This day is Anzac Day!
Made sacred by the memory
Of those who fought and died, and fought and live,
And gave the best that men may give
For love of Land. It dawns once more,
And, though on alien sea and shore
The guns are silent all,
Yet with pride we recall
The deeds which gave immortality.

Great deeds are deathless things!
And doer dies, but not the deed,
And, when upon that fateful April day
Our Anzacs, throwing all but love away,
Gave life and limb for Honour's sake,
With Freedom tremblingly at stake
They lit a beacon-light
Imperishable, bright,
That evermore the Nation's soul shall heed.

Not Peace, not Peace alone
Can make a nation great and good
And bring it that full statute, strength, and grace
That fit it for an age-enduring place

In men's regard. Through storm and strife
It runs to sweet and noble life;
For through its veins there runs
The valour of great sons
Who died to give it stately nationhood.

This day is Anzac Day!
Made sacred by the thrilling thought
Of those who proved their souls, it reappears;
And thus 'twill dawn, and dawn through future years
Till Time our petty deeds efface,
And others, dwelling in our place,
Tell o'er, with tongue and pen,
The glorious tale again
Of how on beach and crags the Anzacs fought.

RECRUITED

W hat the papers said on Wednesday 5 August 1914:
Britain yesterday declared war on Germany and Australia has naturally declared it will join the mother country in defending her shores. Nationalist sentiment is running high with wild enthusiasm and patriotic songs taken up by crowds in the streets.

Down Victoria Parade this mob of 300 larrikins attacked the German Club. They set fire to a piece of rag they proclaimed to be the German flag and yelled abuse until finally the police came and dispersed them.

Prime Minister Mr Joseph Cook pledged to place Australian vessels under the control of the admiralty and offered an expeditionary force of 20,000 men. He said, 'If the Armageddon is to come, then you and I shall be in it . . . if the old country is at war, so are we.'

The leader of the opposition, Mr Andrew Fisher, said on Friday that if war were unavoidable, Australia would defend Britain 'to our last man and our last shilling'.

King George V cabled the people of Australia tonight expressing his appreciation and pride following the dominion's desire to help.

THE CALL

TOM SKEYHILL

Young and old, brave and bold, hark to the clarion call.
Over the rolling seas it comes,
With threat of death and muffled drums,
From fields afar, where shrapnel numbs,
War, War, War!

Big and small, short and tall, hark to the clarion call.
Stay not where the crowd hurrahs,
Speed ye straight to the fields of Mars,
Where red blood flows beneath the stars,
War, War, War!

Mother rare, sweetheart fair, hark to the clarion call.
Slain out there is the peaceful dove,
Rent and torn the heavens above,
Give to the flag the men you love,
War, War, War!

RECRUITED AT THE TOWN HALL

E.F. HANMAN

Eric Hanman (known as 'Haystack' due to his size) fought as a private and landed on 25 April. His writing style is boisterous, energetic and almost childlike at times, yet his grasp of the language and ability to communicate via the written word says a lot for the education system of the day.

His book Twelve Months with the 'Anzacs' *was published in Brisbane in 1916 and included advertisements for products like Nestlé condensed milk. A plea for men to enlist and 'make a sacrifice in the most righteous cause man has ever known' was placed next to an advertisement for Cannon and Cripps Undertakers!*

***

Men lined up outside the recruitment office because our existence was threatened; because we were in danger, our homes, our wives, our children; because England needed us, because we were Britishers, and stood as one. 'Twas enough, 'twas the Call, the call to arms.

But it was at Lismore that the writer found himself on 18 September 1914. Having no home, no friends, no relations, what did it matter where he was? Nothing.

The town itself seemed deserted, save for a few rumbling, grumbling farmers' carts, groaning on their way to some distant little homestead in the bush.

Strolling down one of the sleepy, lazy-looking streets, he suddenly found himself one of a crowd, intent upon the same purpose—that of taking the oath to serve their 'King and Country till the termination of the War and four months after'.

In front of the recruiting hall was a quite respectable crowd consisting of nearly every class and profession. One could easily distinguish the lawyer, the bank clerk, the draper, and the labourer—mostly big, strapping fellows who looked as though they had every chance of becoming food for powder and shot.

In every face could be seen anxiety—anxiety that the owner was suffering from some complaint of which he was unaware—fearful lest he be found unfit. When a chap knows he is to be examined by a medical man, he becomes afraid, he imagines he has a weak heart, lung trouble, or any other of the too numerous diseases which afflict mankind. Assure him as fervently as you like to the contrary, and his brain will run to imaginary complaints until he does feel quite ill. Waiting for the doctor is nearly as bad as awaiting the word of command for a bayonet charge.

Thus every man is sizing up his neighbour and weighing him in the balance when the doctor puts in an appearance. What a relief! What are these chaps with such smart uniforms, such a magnificent martial bearing and such pretty little bits of red and gold spotted on their hats, shoulders, and sleeves? Surely they are Captains; but no, by their voice, and pompous manner, they must surely be no less than Generals! Wait, worried recruit. When you have been in the Army one little week, you will know, only too well, that they are after all only Sergeant Majors on the Instructional Staff.

"Tion, 'tion, 'tion! Look here, you chumps, fall in, fall in, we can't wait here all day, stand over there. No, come over here—that's right, no—damn it—that's wrong. Ah! now fall in.'

Some of us were beginning to think that we had fallen in right enough, but not in the way the drill instructor meant.

Then came the order to strip. What a funny sight!

The doors of the hall were wide open, and a rather fresh breeze blowing in, and there stand or sit in every self-conscious attitude about fifty fellows, all wondering what Adam did in cold weather!

One by one we were called to face the doctor, and it is not exaggeration to state that these same fellows were more frightened then than they were on that never-to-be-forgotten dawn of 25 April 1915.

At last the writer's own turn came. He hopped, jumped, stepped sideways, backwards, forwards, touched toes, waved his arms madly about, so much so that if a stranger appeared he would imagine he was beholding a Salome dance or a rehearsal for a 'corroboree'. He was tapped here, punched there, asked to cough— though that request is superfluous, because if by now you are not coughing, you ought to be. Twiddle round on your heels—very good—the recruit is brought to his senses by 'Halt, about turn'.

You walk forth a soldier whose battles have already commenced, for ten to one someone has admired the pattern of your shirt, and shown a preference for your socks.

DEVIL-MAY-CARE

J.W. GORDON (JIM GRAHAME)

Devil-may-care is on the march, with ever their heads held high;
Theirs is a mighty sacrifice, cheer loud as they're passing by!
Give them a cheer to remember, give them a rousing hand;
Strong and fit, and they'll do their bit, the bravest men in the land.

Shearer's cook and rouseabout, hard-bitten tough of the 'Loo,
Have cobbered up with a parson's son and a freckle-faced jackeroo.
Cream of a nation's manhood, pride of a people's heart,
A Devil-may-care battalion eager to play their part.

Son of a city banker, son of a city slum,
Son of the boundless bushland, keen and alert they come.
Shoulder to shoulder they're marching, hard as steel and as true,
Devil-may-care and reckless—and ready to die or do.

A rollicking hardcase legion—see how the blighters grin!
Those are the kind that are needed, those are the men who'll win.
Swinging to war like their fathers, wiry and ready and game,
The devil-may-cares are marching—on to their deathless fame.

BILL'S RELIGION

WILLIAM BAYLEBRIDGE

Among those questions put to men before we let them into our armed forces, the one that most troubles them is the question that bears upon their creed or religion.

To many men the beliefs of the various church conclaves and synods are dead things of which they know nothing. These men have their own creed, often kept well hidden and containing some strange articles. Some of these articles many a priest, perhaps, would set little store by.

This creed, the creed proper to Australians, we have not yet written down in books, thus, men are at times hard put to answer questions that bear upon their creed or religious beliefs.

There was a young bushman called Bill. He went early to join up for the Light Horse. Having passed the riding test, he was told, with others, to get stripped, and stand in a tent, and wait there till the tape Sergeant called on him. This he did. Seeing him there in his skin only, you could have marked that he was a lengthy lean fellow, broad of bone, with muscle sitting along it like bunched wire. The bush had done that.

Someone said: 'Step forward!' And he stepped up and on to the scale.

'Twelve seven,' said the Sergeant.

He then stood up to have the tape run across him.

'Five eleven and a half—forty—forty-four,' said the Sergeant again.

Then, when they were done with his age, his eyes, the colour of his hair, and the quaint marks, an officer said, looking up: 'What religion?'

Now, this man, because of the reason I have spoken of, could not well answer this.

'My kind,' he said, 'give little thought to that.'

The officer said, 'But, you must tell me this. We require an answer. What belief does your father hold to?'

'He kept it always inside his shirt,' said Bill, slowly, 'no one rightly knew.'

'How, then, was he buried?' asked the officer again, sharply. He did not care much for this man's manners. 'That will clear this thing up.'

'Well,' said Bill, 'the old man had the laugh on them there too, for he put that job through himself.'

'Himself! How so?'

'He dropped down a shaft,' Bill answered, 'and it fell in upon him. This we found out later and, as he was a dead man then, there was nothing left to do but to put the stone up.'

'A poor funeral!' the officer remarked.

'Well, he always said,' answered Bill, 'that he'd care most for a funeral that had little fuss about it.'

The officer, plainly, was losing his patience. 'Have you never heard tell of such things as the Thirty-nine Articles?' he asked, 'the Sermon on the Mount, and the Ten Commandments? Look, my man, don't you know what a Catholic is, and a Quaker? What a Wesleyan is, or a Seventh Day Saint? It might be, now, that you're an Anabaptist,' he said, 'or a Jew. But one of these things you must be. Speak up. The Sergeant has to fill this form in.'

'One of those things I might be,' Bill answered. 'But I can't tell that. I'm a plain man.'

The officer looked at him squarely and then said, with a hard lip, 'Tell me this—have you any religion in you at all?'

'That I can't swear to,' said Bill. 'But an old fellow up our way, who looked after us well as children and often chatted with us around the campfire, said he reckoned so.'

The officer smiled tartly, 'And this bushman had some articles of faith for this religion?'

'He did,' replied Bill.

'This ought to be looked into,' said the officer, 'it may be that he made up the decalogue for it, too.'

'In a manner of speaking he did,' answered Bill again.

'Indeed! And what, then, was that?'

Bill, taking his time about it, said: 'I got this off by heart. To give it in his own words it ran like this:

Honour your country; put no fealty before this.

Honour those who serve it.

Honour yourself; for this is the beginning of all honour.

A mean heart is the starting place of evil.

A clean heart is the dignity of life; keep your heart clean.

Think first; then labour.

Lay to, so that your seed will stand up thick on the earth.

Possess your own soul.

Thou shalt live . . . and

Thou shalt lay down thy life for more life.

'I think that was it,' he said. 'I can't go much into that swagger; but I guess that's about right. Now, if you'll put that question again, I think I could fix it.'

'What, then, is your religion?' asked the officer.

Glad at heart to have found his answer, Bill said, quickly, 'Australian, that's my religion.'

'Well,' said the officer, with a sour smile, 'that will do. Pass on to the doctor.'

On Bill's form, then, in the space against religion, he wrote this word—'None'.

RECRUITED

THOMAS BARKLA

Phyllis, your method of raising recruits
Smacks of the press-gang a trifle.
Here am I wearing impossible boots
And marching about with a rifle
Because you have said
We can never be wed
Until I am carried home, wounded or dead

Now I've a number instead of a name;
The cut of my clothes is atrocious;
Daily I'm drilled until aching and lame,
By officers young and precocious,
Who force me to lie
On my tummy to try
To shoot an imagin'ry bull in the eye.

Please do not think I'm unwilling to go—
I've no intention of quitting;
But, Phyllis, there's one thing I really must know:
For whom is that muffler you're knitting?
I don't care a lot
If by Germans I'm shot:
But if that is for me, I'll desert on the spot!

SAM AND ME

STEELE RUDD

The most notable Australian author to fictionalise the Anzac experience was Arthur Hoey Davis, the famous 'Steele Rudd'.

Davis was born in 1868, in Drayton, near Toowoomba, and worked as a horse breaker, stockman and drover before moving to Brisbane where he began to write poetry and draw sketches for local periodicals.

The first of his stories about selectors appeared in The Bulletin *in 1895 and his many books typically portray life in the Darling Downs area of southern Queensland. His own family were poor selectors and his two main comic creations, Dad and Dave, are among the most famous in Australian literature.*

Davis's fame was so great that he founded his own Steele Rudd's Magazine, *in 1904. His son, Gower, enlisted in 1915 and much of the* Memoirs of Corporal Keeley, *from which the story included here is drawn, is based on Gower's reminiscences. Davis died in 1935.*

***

There were seven of us, all in our teens except Tom Murray and Sam Condle, all sons of cockies and Darling Downs pioneers.

We worked our passage to Blackall, camping a night with Jimmy Power, the big shearer, at the Four Mile Gardens, belonging to a Chinaman, an' helped ourselves to some of his spuds.

From there to Isisford; to Barcaldine; down the Barcoo to Northampton Downs; then to Windorah and across to Adavale where we was heaping up big money when news come that war had broke out with Germany. I don't know how long it was coming but it seemed to have broke out a good while before it reached us.

From Adavale we cut into Charleville, intending to have a good spell there before arranging our next programme.

***

We found Charleville full of nothing but talk and excitement about the war. From what some of them was saying you'd think the Germans had landed and were coming down by Cape York. According to the papers we saw they was all at it, hammer and tongs.

'Australia will be there,' blokes were singing in the street. 'The Empire calls every fit man to the colours' was printed on the walls, an' 'Your country needs your help' was staring at you in the bars.

Blokes was coming in from all parts of the country, selling their horses and belongings an' enlisting, an' some of 'em was blokes Sam an' me met at the sheds. Of course, we got talking to 'em.

'Yer can only get killed once,' they said. 'You got to die some-time, anyhow, an' you'll get a chance to see the blanky world before you do!'

Sam an' me seemed to be the only two that wasn't enlisting.

'We ain't been down to the Post Office yet,' said Sam, the second day we was there, 'to see if any letters come for us.'

Turning our heads around we went down there and the postman gave us a fistful of letters that was plastered all over with 'try Blackall' an' 'try Adavale' an' 'try Isisford' an' goodness knows where else.

I seen the Old Lady's handwriting on one that I got an' stuffed the others in me shirt.

'I'm blowed!' Sam exclaimed, in the middle of one he got from his old man, 'Tom Murray and the other four got home six months ago, an' are going to the war!'

'Eh!?' I fairly squealed, 'to the war!'

'They're in camp in Brisbane,' Sam come in again. He was looking serious as a jew-lizard an' thinking hard to himself.

'Frankie,' he sez, hitching his pants up, 'I'm goin' to enlist; by God, I am!' An', from the look in his eye it would have been Lord help the German that happened to walk into the room at that moment!

'I'll sell the nags here in Charleville,' he said, 'and buy that first-class ticket I always promised meself, then off down to Toowoomba an' enlist there.'

I didn't expect he had anything in his head so good as that!

'Oh, my oath,' I agreed, 'I'm with you in that, all right, an' when we get to Toowoomba I'll see about enlisting too.'

I never knew anyone look so pleased as Sam did when I told him I was goin' to enlist too.

'Good man!' he shouted, an' grabbed me by the hand. 'I knew you'd decide in the confirmative, a bloke like you couldn't do anything else!'

'Of course I couldn't,' I answered, 'I don't think there's much to be afraid of, anyway.'

All the same, I was forced to make a couple of swallers to get rid of a choking feeling that come up into me throat.

***

The Toowoomba platform was crowded when me an' Sam arrived; an' how they all started an' gaped into our carriage as we come backing in.

'There must be a meeting of the Farmers' Union here today,' said Sam, 'look at all the blokes sporting wire whiskers!'

Then we started ducking an' shoving to get through the crowd.

Sam said, 'I never struck a mob like this here before.'

In the street, where there was nothing but cabmen watching us like hawks, we stood and put our heads together for a while and talked things over again.

'I think I'll go straight to the recruiting office and enlist before I change me mind,' Sam says.

Right,' I said, so into town we both goes an' marches up to the recruiting depot.

A lot of chaps same as ourselves was coming out an' goin' into the building when we arrived, most of them waving their hands an' talking about the war an' deciding how to win it.

Looking in the door we saw a couple of blokes in uniform, with stripes on their arms, sitting at a table covered with papers an' pens an' an empty water-bottle.

'There you are, in we go!' says Sam, giving me a shove.

Before I knew where I was the military blokes was pouring questions into me and writing me answers down like lightning.

'Into this room here,' says another in emu feathers and long-necked spurs, 'an' be examined by the doctor.'

In I stumbles, feeling sort of dazed by the imposing surroundings an' more like a bloke that was doomed to be executed before breakfast than a prospective soldier of the King. Cripes! I did get my eyes open all of a sudden, though. For a minute I thought I had got into the swimming baths, then I took it for a blooming asylum.

Here before me was about twenty blokes without a blooming stitch of clothes on, all of 'em naked as skinned kangaroos. Some was bucking round doing high kicks; some pretty old fossils, looking like plucked roosters, was sitting on a bench calmly philosophising on the appearance of the other chaps, an' some more was stalking about putting their chests out and admiring themselves like peacocks.

I looked round for Sam, but he had gone into a different room. So after thinking about it for a while, I started and took me togs off slowly; but not wanting to make a fool of meself altogether I kept me shirt on, an' even with it on I never in me life found meself in such an awkward predicament. A bloke couldn't help feeling downright ashamed of himself and that was all about it. Of course, I squatted on a bench as soon as I could an' pulled me shirt over me knees.

The doctor was putting 'em through one after the other, like a cove shearing with all the shed to himself, an' there was me waiting me turn like the poor old cobbler. Always having an active mind, of course, I got to thinking of the whole damn business again. 'I dunno,' I thought to meself, 'what the devil I wanted coming here for at all.'

'Your turn next,' a bloke sings out to me and disturbs me reflections.

'Oh!' I says, an' jumps up an' move across the room. Passing by a naked recruit he gives me a grin an' pulls up me shirt.

'Steady,' I says, 'none of that.' An' a lot of 'em started laughing.

'Think a bloke hasn't got a bit of respect for himself?' I says to the lot of 'em, an' they laughed more. But I let 'em laugh.

Soon as I face the doctor I began trembling all over an' nearly choked meself pulling at me shirt to make it come down lower. He lifted his eyes from his writing pad an', without bidding a bloke good-day or asking how he was, snaps out, 'Take off your shirt!'

'What, right off?' I says, just to make sure what he meant.

'Yes, yes, what else?' an' he frowns like a burglar.

Back I creeps and chucks the shirt off, an' presents meself to him again with only me pants on.

'Dammit, man!' he blurts out, 'I want to see you with nothing at all on.'

'Oh!' I says, 'can't you examine some of a bloke at a time?'

'Are you married?' he says, an' thinking it was a comical sort of thing to ask a bloke, I grinned.

'Are you?' he barks, stamping his foot.

'Not yet,' I says, with another grin.

'And I don't think you ever will be,' he says.

Then, turning to the chap in the emu feathers and the long-necked spurs, he says, 'For God's sake, take the pants off this innocent abroad and let me get to my work!'

'Whip 'em off, everyone does it!' says the Captain or whatever he was, striding for me as if he meant to tear 'em off me.

'Oh, orright,' I says, 'if everyone does it I'll do it.'

Then, turning me back on 'em I lets down me pants an' was bending low getting me foot outa the leg, when that infernal Captain brought me the most terrific spank I ever heard, with his open hand! Cripes, I nearly hit the ceiling with me head!

'Oy, steady!' I says to him, 'I didn't come here for that sort of thing!'

When the doctor stopped laughing he steps over to me and says, 'Why, a man made like you ought to be only too proud to show yourself naked. You're the best built youngster I ever saw in my life.'

That changed me feelings an' me opinion of him in a second.

'Do you think so?' I says, forgetting the pain and me nakedness an' grinning proudly.

'I'm sure of it.'

Then he starts tapping me chest and putting his ear to me and pulling me about.

'Hmmm,' he says, an' looks into me mouth, as if I was a horse he was buying.

Then, to see if I ever went to school, he asks me to read the blooming ABC. Cripes, it was easy as snuff.

'Pass!' says the Captain.

'Wish we could get another hundred thousand like him,' says the doctor. Then, putting his hand on me shoulder, he says to me, 'Sound as a bell, me boy. Good luck to you, and see you come back with a V.C.'

Outside I found Sam waiting for me already, with a broad smile on him.

'How did you get on?' he asked.

'Good,' I answered, an' started laughing. Then he started laughing, an' we both went out the gate roaring laughing.

***

We went into camp at Enoggera, an' into dungarees an' a white rag hat and big boots that were a load to carry. Lord! Sam an' me did look a pair but one couldn't laugh at the other which was the only satisfaction about it.

For the first couple of days we thought it the maddest place we ever got into, an' the maddest lot of blokes we ever struck. The camp was all tents an' buildings an' sheds an' big holes in the ground an' trenches dug crooked an' big stumps half grubbed out. It looked like a goldfield.

Thousands of us blokes separated into different mobs was kept running about, on an' off, on an' off all day, drilling. When we wasn't drilling we was shooting at targets or digging, or anything else that wasn't of much use. An' talk about Colonels an' Lieutenant Colonels and Majors an' Captains an' Sergeants. That was the place to see those gentlemen. They was as plentiful as kangaroos was in the bush. Everywhere you turned you met two or three of 'em swinging canes, an' to hear 'em giving orders was better than listening to an auctioneer selling poor horses.

Cripes! I never knew what a small inconsequential bloke I was till I got into that camp. There was even a parson there that me an' Sam run into once out at Blackall, stalking about in a uniform with leggings up to his knees.

'Well, I'm blowed,' says Sam the first time we saw him, 'surely he ain't goin' to the blooming war, too?' An' both of us burst out laughing.

'What's up with you fellows?' a Sergeant coming in for his dinner says.

We told him what the joke was and expected he'd join in it with us, but he didn't.

'That's Lieutenant Colonel Chaplain Brown-Smith,' he says, 'and he goes to the front with the next Division.'

'But we met that bloke once,' Sam told him, 'about forty miles out of Blackall, crawling along on a blessed old moke that you wouldn't give a feed to.'

'I don't care if you met him four mile outside of hell!' the Sergeant barked, 'you might meet him outside the trenches and be damn glad to, too! An' don't let me tell both of you again,' he added in his own interests, 'to salute your officers wherever you meet them.' An' suiting the word to the action he give us a demonstration.

Me an' Sam grinned an' give him one back, but by mistake lifted the wrong hand. Then he lifted his voice an' swore an' reckoned it was only wasting breath talking to blokes like us.

We shared a good tent along with some other recruits to camp in, but no bunks, so it was scratch the chips an' pebbles away an' sleep on the ground. But me an' Sam was used to that. When 'lights out' was sounded by the bugler we turned in as regular as clockwork, but we was there a long time before we could get into the habit of falling off to sleep.

Instead of the tinkle-tonkle of horse-bells an' the screaming of the curlews an' the howling of the dingoes, the voice of the officer drilling us kept ringing in our ears all night an' keeping us awake.

***

The route marches to the seaside agreed with us though. Sam an' me was pretty good at marching, we got plenty of practice at it going to the Barcoo, when we lost our horses, which I didn't tell you about.

Some of the city blokes didn't take too kindly to marching though an' used to drop out along the road to have a spell. A great sight was the sea for the first time, Sam an' me couldn't take our eyes off it. Lord, it only wanted a bit of saltbush or a mulga tree sticking out of it here and there an' we would have reckoned we was on the edge of the Western Plains again.

'That's where we'll be going pretty soon I suppose,' Sam says, 'right across there to blazes . . . anywhere.' An' both of us folded our arms an' looked out as far as we could see to what seemed to be the end of the world. An' to many of those brave fellows shouting and romping there in the waves that day, it surely was.

The day we got our uniform, an' flung the dungarees an' old rag hat into a corner, was the day of our lives.

'Jeemimah!' Sam says, standing up in the tent, 'how the devil do I look in 'em, Frankie?'

'Holy war!' I says, 'you're all right. How do I look meself?' An' I marched around grinning at him.

'Cripes,' he says, 'if I look half as good as you I'm satisfied!'

I was six foot two, you know, an' a bit heavier than Sam.

'We must apply for home leave at once,' he says, 'an' go straight home an' show ourselves to everyone. Lord Nelson an' the Duke of Wellington was never in it with us, Frankie!'

I agreed with Sam on that count.

About a week later we got our leave an' off we goes without letting anyone know we was coming. But before we left we was told by the O.C. that we would be leaving for the front in eight days an' that we had to make our wills an' settle our private affairs.

That was a shock that was.

'Wills!' I gasped at Sam. 'Cripes!'

It took all the sport outa soldiering for me an' somehow I couldn't look forward to enjoying meself at home at all . . . not after that.

'There's nothing in making your will, Frankie,' Sam said soothingly, 'everybody makes 'em whether they goes to the war or whether they doesn't.'

'Oh, I know that,' I answered, shrugging me shoulders an' trying to grin. But I nearly strangled meself trying to swaller the same infernal lump that was forever coming into me throat. 'I was just thinking it's hardly worth a bloke's while.'

Anyhow we got home all right an' didn't we cause a sensation!

Four days we had of home leave an' a dance was held every night at some of the places in honour of Sam an' me. Wristlet watches was presented to the two of us an' three cheers was called for us, but I couldn't get the will business an' the thoughts of goin' to the front out of me head for a minute, they stuck there like bullets. An' when the morning came to leave I sat on the bed holding me uniform in me hands wondering for long enough if I ought to put it on again or not.

Lots gathered to see us off, an' they all shook hands with me, some of 'em more than once, an' others kissed me for the first time in their lives, an' Connie Crutch whispered into me ear, 'Be sure an' write often, Frankie, an' come back safe.'

An' then I . . . I . . . well, it don't matter what I did, now.

***

I was seasick nearly all the way round the coast an' took little interest in anything that went on, an' cared less. Leaving West Australia I stood on the deck beside Sam, a bit away from the rest of the soldiers, watching an' watching.

It was a strange feeling I had just then, an' it seemed to be shared by all the others. The cheering they gave us as we moved out died away, an' the cheering we gave 'em back died away. Hats an' handkerchiefs kept waving at intervals. The rays from the setting sun skimmed the top of the waves an' volumes of black smoke rolled from the funnels of the line of transports following behind an' melted into the sea.

Every man there seemed silent as the grave an' all kept watching for a last glimpse of their native land. Smaller an' smaller, dimmer an' dimmer the coast of Australia became; for a little while just a speck remained visible, an' then . . .

'That's the last some of us will ever see of her,' I heard one soldier say. An' if he had run a knife into me heart he couldn't have dispirited me more than he did.

'It's seasickness, that's all it is, old chap,' Sam said, helping me down below an' seeing me into me bunk.

I was in that bunk pretty well all the way to Egypt, feeling down if ever a bloke was in this world. 'Damned if I can understand you at all,' the doctor said to me several times.

But I could understand meself well enough an' day after day I kept repeating the same useless reproach, 'Why did you enlist? Oh, why did you enlist?'

When we reached Alexandria I took Sam's advice an' pulled meself together an' did me best to forget what might or might not happen in the future. 'Who the hell cares?' I said to meself, fighting against it, an' when the sand of the desert got into me socks, an' me hair, an' me ears an' me eyes an' me mouth, I just laughed when the others was all swearing, an' went about whistling.

All the same, when we got to Cairo an' the pyramids an' all them places, I hadn't the desire for exploring an' sight-seeing that the others had. It wasn't that I hadn't plenty of money, either, because I had. But, whenever I was off duty, I put in me time writing to the old people, an' Connie Crutch, an' lying down just thinking an' thinking.

When we was finally leaving Egypt for Lemnos, an' Sam an' all the others was wildly excited about it, I sat down an' wrote what I thought would be me last letter home, telling 'em that our Division was on the move an' I didn't expect they'd ever see me again.

Mudros, when we arrived there, was alive with warships an' boats. On Mudros there was a lot of old houses, an' old gardens, an' what looked like a church, an' some wild flowers . . . an' that's all I remember of what it looked like. But the cheer after cheer we got from the French ships an' the Tommies as we steamed into that harbour I will remember till the day I die.

'By God, Frankie,' said poor old Sam, 'that was worth coming all the way from Australia for, if nothing else was!'

ALL THE WAY FROM AUSTRALIA

JIM HAYNES

'Cheer, cheer, the red and the white . . .'
I'm belting out the Sydney Swans victory song as we travel along the highway from Bursa, ancient capital of the Ottoman Empire, to the ferry station on the shore of the Sea of Marmara.

There are four of us driving back to Istanbul after a week on the road and the mood in the Mercedes minibus is one of comradeship and joviality. Two of us are Australian—my wife, Robyn, and me—and two are Turkish—Ali, our guide, and Mehemet, our driver.

Mehemet is a small, wiry, bright-eyed man for whom nothing is ever a problem. He smiles and laughs a lot and smokes too much. We measure the time we spend exploring any one place by the number of cigarettes Mehemet smokes while he waits for us. At some places he jokes and says that we stopped so long to look and explore that we are seriously damaging his health!

Although he has little English, Mehemet is easy to communicate with and understand; he is a man of gestures and single words. A family man, proud of his clever daughter who is top in her year at the all-girls school she attends in Istanbul, Mehemet is keen to tell us about her when he discovers Robyn is a teacher at an all-girls school in Sydney.

Like me, Mehemet is also a racing enthusiast, and Ali has been kept busy translating between us as we attempt to explain the subtleties of Australian and Turkish horseracing to each other.

Ali is a wonderful guide—companionable, well educated, efficient and hospitable. He is proud of his country and keen to help us experience all facets of its culture and history. At the same time, he has a good grasp of the realities of Turkey's place in the world and the problems his nation still faces. With his encyclopaedic mind, he is the perfect guide for the curious, open-minded traveller.

Ours is a private tour and Ali is always accommodating and flexible. If we wish to spend extra time anywhere, or revisit certain places, as we did on the Gallipoli Peninsula several days earlier, Ali simply makes it happen with a smile. If we miss the regular ferry in order to spend more time on research, Ali always knows the place where the smaller ferry leaves.

As an added bonus, Ali also has a gourmet's knowledge of every town and village, and seems to know the culinary specialities of every region and restaurant in Turkey. We have eaten very well in Turkey and it has been a satisfying and well-rounded trip, in more ways than one. We have been met everywhere with typical Turkish courtesy and hospitality, and extra friendliness every time we are introduced as Australians.

***

When we are not discussing history or the Gallipoli campaign or food, we discuss other things of universal interest, like football.

As Mehemet steers us along the crowded highway, Ali is busy telling me how most right-thinking Turkish football supporters detest the silvertails of Turkish football, Fenebache. Any sensible Turkish football fan, he assures me, supports his own team and the one that's playing against Fenebache. I tell him that in Australian football we all support our own team and the one that is playing against Collingwood.

Ali and Mehemet both live in Besiktas, the old naval port area of Istanbul, and consequently they support Besiktas Football Club. Over the past week they have sung quite a few Turkish folksongs during long hauls between cities and now they sing a few Besiktas Football Club supporters' songs. Most Turkish men love to sing, and can sing quite well.

I tell Ali that most Australian men don't sing in the normal course of daily events and singing is pretty much confined to the supporters of the winning side at the very end of an AFL game. Nevertheless, I sing the Sydney Swans song for them.

When I finish my raucous rendition, I point out that the Turkish national colours of red and white are also the Swans' colours. Ali says that he will now become a Swans supporter whenever he meets other Australians.

THE BATTLE OF CANAKKALE– 18 MARCH 1915

JIM HAYNES

In 1908 a group of students and military officers known as the Young Turks led a revolt against Sultan Abdulhamit and then ruled the Ottoman Empire using his brother, Mehmet V, as a puppet sultan.

Not long after World War I began, the Ottoman Empire was lured into an alliance with the Central Powers, partly through the ruling committee's leader, Enver Pasha, having a German background and sympathies, and partly due to Russia being the Ottoman Empire's old and obvious enemy.

The Germans convinced the Ottomans to close the Dardanelles, the waterway between the Aegean Sea and the Black Sea, thereby blocking the sea route to southern Russia and preventing Allied arms and supplies being sent to the Eastern Front.

An appeal by the Russian government to the British War Office and high command prompted the Allied decision to attack the Dardanelles.

Russian troops were being hard-pressed in the Caucasus and the Allies hoped that a British attack might cause the Ottomans to withdraw. They also hoped to open a supply route to Russia by 'forcing the Dardanelles'.

It is generally acknowledged that the fall of Constantinople would have been a foregone conclusion had the Allied fleet passed through the Narrows.

French and British warships attacked Turkish forts at Cape Helles and along the Straits in February and March 1915. They encountered underwater mines, torpedoes, and spirited defence and artillery bombardment from the Turkish forts along the shores of the Dardanelles at the Narrows, near the Turkish town of Canakkale.

On 18 March 1915 the British and French fleets attempting to force the Straits suffered a humiliating defeat, losing six battleships. British losses were the *Irresistible* and the *Ocean* sunk in the Narrows, and the *Inflexible* was crippled and run ashore at Tenedos. The French lost the *Bouvet*, sunk in the Narrows, and the *Gaulois*, beached on a tiny island back towards Lemnos, while the *Suffren* was badly damaged and retired.

March 18 is a national day in Turkey. Although it was technically the Ottoman Empire, as Germany's ally, which was at war with France and Britain, the defeat of the British and French fleets at the Battle of Canakkale was a very 'Turkish' victory and is considered to be the first step in the establishment of the Turkish nation.

THE LANDING

The Australian and New Zealand Army Corps was a combined force of Australian and New Zealand volunteer soldiers. The corps was formed in Egypt during 1914 and was led by the British general William Birdwood.

After the naval attack on the Dardanelles failed, the British military leader at Gallipoli, General Sir Ian Hamilton, conferred with the Sea Lords and Field Marshal Horatio Kitchener and it was decided that a naval action would not succeed without an invasion in force by infantry. Plans were immediately made for a massive invasion to try to seize the Gallipoli Peninsula.

At the time, the arrival at Gallipoli was the largest military landing in history. It involved about 75,000 men from the United Kingdom, France, Australia, New Zealand, Nepal and India. After several postponements due both to poor weather and to a mix-up loading some of the supply ships, the huge flotilla sailed from the Allied base on the island of Lemnos on 24 April 1915. The landings began before dawn the following day.

The main Allied force, consisting of British and French troops, landed at five different locations at Cape Helles, on the tip of the peninsula.

The ANZAC force of about 30,000 men was to be landed at Gaba Tepe, more than 16 kilometres north of Helles, but actually landed even further north in an area later called Anzac Cove. On the first day, 16,000 Anzac troops went ashore, the majority of them going into battle for the first time.

RED GALLIPOLI

H.W. CAVILL

We were roused before 6 a.m. by the rattle of the anchor cable, and, by the time we had scrambled on deck, we were gliding down the placid waters of Mudros Bay. We could hardly believe our luck. After eight strenuous months' training, we were at last on the move and, before many hours, should realise to the full what war meant.

Winding our way through the throng of ships, we quickly approached the mouth of the Bay—passing, as we steamed out, the monster battleships *Queen Elizabeth*, *London*, *Prince of Wales* and *Queen*, while sleek, business-like destroyers darted hither and thither.

Passing the heads and the peaceful-looking little lighthouse, we steamed slowly round the island and dropped anchor again in a small cove on the opposite side. Here business began in earnest; iron rations were distributed; arms and equipment inspected; in fact, everything possible to secure success was attended to.

My! Didn't I grin when I saw the ship's grindstone. The boys were afraid their bayonets would not be sharp enough, so there they were, gathered around waiting eagerly their turn to get at the stone. By the time we left the ship it was gouged and worn to such an extent that it was fit for nothing but a kellick stone.

As I sit up here on the boat-deck writing these lines, it is hard to believe that within a few hours we shall be in the midst of slaughter and suffering. As I sit and look around, all is peace and beauty. The setting sun floods the dancing water and casts its rays over the beautiful green hills of Lemnos, the quaint little windmills completing a sweet picture. But it is work that has to be accomplished, so we look to Him who has been our help in ages past.

The boys were entirely unconcerned; they lay about the decks absorbed in cards, reading, and so forth. Evening found them in the same good spirits, and a happy, rollicking time was spent. One thing, only, pointed to the fact that something unusual was happening. Before retiring, every man packed his valise with extra care; poised his rifle to an electric light and had a final squint through; then finally lay down, still in jocular mood.

I do not profess to know if it is the correct thing to sleep blissfully on the eve of a battle, especially such a battle as we were faced with, but this I do know, what within half an hour the ship was filled with the harmonious melody of a multitude of contented sleepers.

I was still enjoying that blissful period that comes on one just before fully waking. Events were taking shape in my mind; I had just become aware, by the even throb of the engines and the motion of the ship, that we were moving, when to my ears came a sound of distant thunder that swelled louder and louder, in a mighty crescendo, punctuated by terrific crashes as if the very heavens were falling.

You can easily guess I was fully awake by this time, and shouting 'We are there' I flew up the companion-way and on to deck. Already there were a few on deck, but there was little to be seen. The morning mist shrouded everything, and one could only judge the position of the land by the flash of the shore batteries as they returned the fire of the fleet.

Steadily we continued our way, passing battleships in action every few minutes. One after another they would loom up out of the impenetrable grey, deafen us with their mighty guns, and then, as we steamed on, disappear like phantom ships into the gloom. At last we dropped anchor close to two of our ships that could only be located by the flash of their guns.

It was a queer sight—on every hand these darting flames, followed by ear-splitting explosions, while every moment the leaden-coloured water would rise in a mighty column, like some magnificent fountain, as the shells from the shore plunged in.

Slowly the mist of the early morn lifted, and there before our eyes lay a scene such as I never dare hope to witness a second time in this life. I could hardly drag myself away to dress; but, at last, slipping into my clothes and putting the last touches to my equipment, I quickly got into a position where I could watch the mighty effort of the Fleet.

We occupied the extreme left of the position. Round about us lay scores of troopships, trawlers, destroyers, and warships. Standing out prominently among the latter was the old H.M.S. *Euryalus*, so well known in Australia a few years ago as our navy's flagship. She was right inshore, and engaged at point-blank range the formidable Gaba Tepe battery, which had been doing serious damage, enfilading the beach.

The terrific duel that ensued made everything else appear trivial. The water about the *Euryalus* was churned into foam, and flew up in great columns, but the old ship doggedly hung to her position, while her gunners simply drove us into a frenzy of cheering, as, with marvellous exactness, they dropped shell after shell on to the position.

For over twenty minutes the scrap continued; till finally this piece of landscape lost all shape, the battery was silenced, and the forces no doubt retreated, for the guns were trained to throw the shells, first over the headland, then right up and over the first gradient.

One could hardly believe that at any moment the boys were under fire of the shore batteries. They filled the rigging and decks, and at every salvo from the warships a mighty cheer would rend the air, and then the ship would ring with laughter. No, there were no long faces, but rather a joyous, reckless fearlessness that boded ill for their foes.

The spasmodic crackle of rifle fire now grew into one continuous roll, like the beating of a thousand kettle drums; the 3rd Brigade were getting busy. But, hark!

'Fall in, A and B Companies.'

Swiftly, the eager waiters stepped into their places, and then just as quickly slipped over the ship's side and down the rope ladders, entirely forgetful of the seventy-odd pound load of equipment they carried.

The crews of the destroyers on each side of the ship worked like Trojans, packing the men in like the proverbial sardines, while we of C and D Companies, who were to go by the second tow, wriggled out of portholes at the risk of cracking our necks, and shouted, 'Jack, I say, Jack, how's things ashore? How did the boys go?'

Thus they rattled on in disjointed conversation, just as the pressure of business would allow.

At last, after what seemed an eternity, our turn came and with the eagerness of school children off for a picnic, we scrambled down the ladders and into the destroyer *Usk*. Scarcely had we left the *Derfflinger* than we heard a high whining noise.

A land battery had opened fire on her, and shell after shell came screaming overhead and plunged all round our recent home.

It was a nerve-trying time. Our destroyer raced toward the beach, escaping in a miraculous manner the storm of shrapnel. Within a few hundred yards of the shore the destroyer eased down; quickly we jumped into the ship's boats that were being towed alongside; and, with a hearty hurrah, gave way and rowed through the curtain of fire that enveloped the beach.

The question has been asked many times, 'What did you feel like when first under fire?'

I have already described our feelings when leaving the ship; but, as we drew nearer the shore, lips were set, faces grew stern and thoughtful, rifles were gripped more firmly, hands stole quietly round and loosened bayonets, and then—then nothing else to do, and being 'Real Australians', the lads once again joked and laughed, yes actually laughed.

As the keel of the boat grated on the rocky bottom, one and all jumped waist deep into the sea and waded ashore, still quite merry, in spite of the hail of shrapnel that bespattered the beach.

No sooner had we gained the shore than the first man was killed. Not five yards from where I stood a C Company man was struck in the head by a splinter of a shell that burst right in our midst; fortunately nobody else was hit.

We were now in the thick of business. Immediately the 1st, 2nd and 3rd Battalions were ordered to advance to support the covering party.

Dropping our packs, the 2nd Battalion rushed at once to the left flank, where a handful of the covering party were hotly engaged. Then came a toilsome scramble over the high bluffs, carrying, in addition to our equipment, picks, shovels, and boxes of ammunition.

Reaching the top of the first ridge, we came to a Turkish trench, in which lay those Turks who had stayed too long to dispute possession with the 3rd Brigade. Stooping low, we doubled across a plateau over which the sharp-nosed bullets flew, meowing like motherless kittens. A constant stream of wounded men—still quite cheerful—passed us on the way to the beach, saying, 'It's hot as hell up there'—and it was.

All down through Shrapnel Valley, thick with mines and pitfalls, infested with snipers, and torn with shrapnel—from whence it earned its name—hairbreadth escapes were now becoming so frequent that one scarcely stopped to notice them.

We commenced fighting our way up the third hill which, personally, I think was the worst of the lot. Never again do I expect to see such superhuman efforts. Dragging the ammunition and entrenching implements, the men struggled up this almost perpendicular, crumbling, scrub-covered cliff in the face of a withering fire.

One exposed knoll, which the snipers were paying particular attention to, we were compelled to rush over singly. As it came to my turn, I bolted, pick in one hand and rifle in the other, as hard as my legs would carry me. One had simply to claw one's way up the soft, yielding bank. No sooner had I reached the top than a dozen bullets kicked up the dirt all around me. An officer who followed me said, 'What's the matter, laddie?'

'Drop,' I shouted.

He did so, only just in time to miss a perfect fusillade of snipers' bullets.

Side by side we wriggled over the knoll, slid down the opposite side, regained our feet, and put up a record sprint to where the rugged hill afforded some little cover.

At the top of the hill we were in the full blast of the enemy's fire. It was a perfect inferno. A score of machine-guns filled the air with their rat-a-tat; just like a hundred noisy motor bicycles; while the Turkish artillery threw a curtain of shrapnel along the ridge that looked as if it would stop any further effort to advance. But, knowing that our only safety lay in victory, one had to forget self and fight like the very devil.

Many of the boys never passed that shrapnel-swept ridge. One wounded lad, who was bleeding badly over the shoulder, propped himself up as we passed, and grinning hideously with his shattered mouth, he wheezed, 'Got it where the chicken got the axe,' then fainted.

Right and left men were being hit, and a fellow had to just clench his teeth and keep going, with the vague thought somewhere in the back of your cranium that you might be the next. It was just here that my chum, Howard Proctor, was killed.

A shrapnel burst right in the midst of the platoon in front of me; it cut the haversack from the side of Corporal Turton, and splashed two or three others, but poor Proctor was struck with a piece of the shell, which inflicted a fatal wound. The lads close at hand, after shaking hands with him, offered a few words of cheer, and then had to advance.

A few minutes later, when my platoon advanced, I knelt by his side, but he was going fast; I tried to cheer him, but somehow I got a big lump in my throat, my eyes were dimmed, and after a few incoherent words I was silent. Then, in spite of the fact that he was paralysed by his wound, and almost at his last gasp, his face brightened, and with a smile he said, 'Don't worry about me, Cav; I feel quite satisfied; I feel I have done my bit; take my glasses and try and return them to my mother.' And so brave Proctor passed away.

Can you wonder, reader, that we old boys of the 1st Brigade reverence the very name of Anzac?

When we remember the number of our hero chums that sleep the long sleep on the bleak, forbidding hills above Anzac Cove, well have they been named 'The Glorious Dead'.

Can we ever forget the unselfish spirit of soldiers like Pte. W. Penton. Mortally wounded, face downward he lay. Yet, with his last effort, and his last breath, he raised himself, and turning to a mate, said, 'Good-bye, Warrington, old boy; I'm going; but tell Albert he will find plenty of cigarettes in my pack.'

Upon uttering those words, poor Penton fell forward and he was gone.

His parents weep and mourn, but we who knew him will ever cherish the memory of such a great, unselfish soul. No words are there more true than those of Souter, when he said: *'We need no costly monument to keep their memory fast.'*

I trust I shall be forgiven if I tell of the heroism of yet another before I pick up the thread of my story.

It is the story of Sgt. Larkin, the member for Willoughby in the NSW Legislative Assembly. He lay wounded and dying and yet when the stretcher-bearers came to carry him in, he waved them on, saying, 'There's plenty worse than me out there.' Later, they found him—dead.

Can anyone feel surprised when we get in a rage at the sight of ham and beef shops branded 'ANZAC'?

The splendid courage of our officers compelled admiration. Separated from their own men—for in the wild fighting over the hills the 1st Brigade was quite mixed up—they gathered all the men in sight, and, with commendable courage, charged the enemy's position with the bayonet.

It was in this way that I was separated from my own Company, and fought throughout the day alongside of Major B.I. Swannell, who, with his Company, had got mixed up with our Battalion.

Never shall I forget the look on his face when we first got within striking distance of the enemy.

'Fix bayonets! Charge!' rang out his order.

There was a flash of steel, a wild hurrah, and the boys dashed straight at the wall of fire, heedless of the frightful slaughter. They were not to be stopped.

It was in this charge that Major Swannell was killed. He had seized a rifle, and with dauntless courage was leading his men, when a Turkish bullet, penetrating his forehead, ended his career, thus depriving the 1st Brigade of one of its bravest officers.

The few remaining hours of daylight were spent in such fierce, unequal fighting that I remembered little else until, about an hour before dusk, something hit me.

I thought at first that I had been struck by a shell. After picking myself up, and regaining a sitting position, I put my hand down to feel if my leg was still there; I was really scared to look, for fear it had gone. Feeling that that really useful member was still attached to my body, I started to discover the extent of the damage. Whipping off my puttee and slashing the seam of my breeches with my clasp knife, I reached my knee, to find a small, quite respectable looking puncture close alongside the knee-cap, from which oozed a thin stream of blood.

The bullet—for such it was—had gone right through, coming out behind the knee, severing, en route, some of the important nerves of the leg, thus paralysing the leg. This was temporarily useful, as it saved me any intense pain.

It was just at this stage that the Turks, heavily reinforced, counter-attacked, and compelled our sadly diminished force to fall back. I knew that if I jumped to my feet to retire I would only collapse, as my leg was as useless as though there was no bone in it.

The only thing to avoid capture was to crawl, and crawl pretty quickly.

So, on one knee and two hands, I started, faced with a three-mile journey over as rough country as it would be possible to find.

How I accomplished the distance safely I shall never know. At least a dozen snipers wasted a cartridge on me—the bullets clipping twigs in front of my nose, whistling through my hair, and kicking the dirt up in my face.

On one occasion a platoon of Australians passed on their way to the firing line. One man, dropping out, half carried me back about a hundred yards, and, with a sincere, 'Good luck, mate,

I'm needed up above,' he raced away to assist the hard-pressed, exhausted men in the firing line.

So again I started off, crawling as hard as possible. While lying on my back, resting in one place, eight or nine shells burst in quick succession right over my head—one bursting so close that the black soot, like burnt powder, fell on my chest. The shrubs were torn and the earth scarred by the hail of shrapnel bullets, but again I got off without a scratch.

I came to the hurried conclusion, however, that there were many healthier places about, and made off again.

I had gone only a short distance when I came upon a touching spectacle. I was crossing a narrow road on the summit of a hill when I saw an officer sitting upright on the roadside, with his back to the shrubs that grew on either side.

I approached, but he did not speak or move, so I crawled up close, and found to my surprise that he was dead. He had just been in the act of writing when a bullet through the heart caused instantaneous death. He had never moved an inch; his notebook was still in the left hand; while the right still held a pencil poised in a natural position over the book. He was a Colonel, past middle age, grey-haired, and wearing a breast full of service ribbons.

In a shallow trench close by another pathetic incident occurred. Lying in a trench was an Australian, who had been badly hit. His eyes opened slowly, his lips moved, and faintly he murmured, 'Mafeesh', the Arabic for 'finished', and more slowly, 'Take money-belt—missus and kids—dirty swap dirty . . .' Then a strange thing happened. Dying, shattered beyond recognition, he rose to his knees and dragged his rifle to the parapet. With a weak finger he took shaky aim and fired his last shot, then collapsed in the bottom of the trench.

A little later I had another very narrow escape. I was crawling along, dragging a rifle which I had picked up in case I met any stray Turks, when right before me, at no distance, I spotted a rifle poking through a shrub, and behind it a New Zealander in the act of pulling trigger. 'Don't fire; I'm wounded,' I yelled and immediately a New Zealand officer jumped out from behind the bush. He was just rushing a company of infantry to reinforce the line.

'Where's the firing line?' he asked.

'Straight on, over a mile ahead of you,' I answered.

With a 'Sorry you're hurt, my boy!' he rushed his men on.

After escapes innumerable, and a struggle that I never expected to accomplish, I reached the ridge of the first hill in company with a New Zealander, who was also wounded. Together we hopped and stumbled, with our arms about one another's neck, finally rolling over the brow of the hill into a hole that afforded some little amount of shelter.

We settled down there for a short spell before continuing to the dressing station on the beach. The wounded still passed in apparently endless procession. They were wonderfully cheerful and full of information. But here our peace was short-lived.

Gradually the enemy's range lengthened, and shells crept nearer and nearer; machine-gun and rifle fire commenced to whisk about us again; then suddenly through the scrub broke the head remnant of the firing line.

Slowly they came, disputing every inch and reluctantly yielding the ground which they had so gloriously occupied during the earlier hours of the day.

The Turks evidently intended to drive them into the sea by sheer weight of numbers, but they were determined to die rather than surrender the position dearly won. Having retired some little distance in an orderly manner, they concentrated on the ring of hills commanding the beach, and, hastily entrenching, prepared to meet the massed infantry that were being hurled forward.

They had not long to wait, for very soon the whole ridge was black with Turks. On they came, evidently thinking that very soon they would sweep the remnant of our little force from their shores. But they were sadly mistaken.

When they were within easy range, a storm of rifle and machine-gun fire tore lanes through their massed ranks, while the *Queen Elizabeth*, which had been unable to support us during the afternoon, opened fire with her fifteen-inch guns, causing fearful losses.

The Turks were stunned by such a reception, and retired over the hill, giving the boys time to further consolidate the position; but they came again and again, meeting with the same withering fire each time.

Eventually they retired for the night, leaving the gallant survivors in peace, and in possession of the joyful thought that they had come through the severest fighting, and 'had done their bit'.

Thus ended the memorable 25 April 1915, 'The Day' . . . on which 16,000 Anzacs won for Australasia an 'Imperishable Record' and a 'Name among all the Nations'.

SONG OF THE DARDANELLES

HENRY LAWSON

From the southern hills and the city lanes,
From the coastal towns and the Blacksoil Plains;
Australia's finest—there they stood,
To fight for the King as we knew they would.
    Knew they would—
    Knew they would;
To fight for the King as we knew they would.

They trained in the dust of an old dead land
Long months of drill in the scorching sand;
But they knew in their hearts it was for their good,
And they saw it through as we knew they would.
    Knew they would—
    Knew they would;
And they saw it through as we knew they would.

They were shipped like sheep when the dawn was grey;
And as the ships left Mudros Bay
They squatted and perched where'er they could,
And they laughed and swore as we knew they would.
    Knew they would—
    Knew they would;
They laughed and swore as we knew they would.

The wireless tells and the cable tells
How our boys behaved by the Dardanelles.
Some thought in their hearts, 'Will our boys make good?'
We knew them of old and we knew they would!
    Knew they would—
    Knew they would;
They were mates of old and we knew they would.

The sea was hell and the shore was hell,
With mine, entanglement, shrapnel and shell,
But they stormed the heights as Australians should,
And they fought and they died as we knew they would.
    Knew they would—
    Knew they would;
They fought and they died as we knew they would.

BIRDWOOD

JIM HAYNES

William Riddell Birdwood was commander of the Australian troops throughout World War I. It is said that he was the only high-ranking British officer who could have successfully led Australian soldiers.

He was born in 1865 in Pune (Poona), India. His father was under-secretary to the government of Bombay, and William was educated at Clifton College, Bristol, and the Royal Military College, Sandhurst, England. Originally posted to the 12th Lancers in India, he later served with the 11th Bengal Lancers. In 1894 he married a baron's daughter, Jeannette Hope Gonville.

Prior to 1914 he served in various North-West Frontier campaigns and in the Boer Wars as part of Lord Kitchener's staff in South Africa. He became major general in 1911 and was secretary to the Army Department in India.

In November 1914 Lord Kitchener, as minister for war, gave Birdwood, aged fifty, command of the ANZAC forces. Right from the start he adopted a friendly, tolerant approach to the Australians he commanded, and the diggers generally respected and liked him.

At Anzac he spent time every day visiting the front trenches and chatting to the men, and there are many stories about his relationship with the troops he commanded. One oft-told story is that he would never accept a drink of water while up on the firing line, as he knew that men had to carry every pint of water up from the beach.

Although he neither smoked nor drank, the Aussies loved his friendly attitude and the fact that he yarned with them and never bothered if they saluted or not. He swam every day with the men and loved telling the story of how, on one occasion when shrapnel was bursting over the beach, an Aussie soldier pushed him under the water as he swam and yelled, 'Get your head down, you silly old dill!'

He was the only senior officer opposed to the evacuation, yet it was he who planned and led the brilliant evacuation operations at Suvla, Anzac Cove and Helles, which were all evacuated without loss in December and January. He took command of the Australian Imperial Force (AIF) in France in March 1916.

Birdwood was given three knighthoods after the war, and was created a baronet and granted £10,000 in 1919. He became Field Marshal and Commander-in-Chief of the Indian Army in 1925.

When Birdwood retired in 1930, King George V wanted to appoint him as Australia's Governor General, but Scullin, the prime minister at the time, insisted on an Australian and Isaac Isaacs was appointed instead. Birdwood became Master of Peterhouse College, Cambridge, in 1931 and, in 1938, was made Baron Birdwood of Anzac and Totnes.

His name is still revered in Australia and a town in South Australia is named after him.

In September 1915 he wrote in a letter home, 'I feel completely Australian.'

Of the many stories about 'Birdie's' affection for his men, this one is my favourite.

Towards the end of the war a group of British staff officers accompanied Birdwood on a tour of a quiet stretch of the defences at Le Touquet, in France.

When an Australian sentry failed to either salute or acknowledge the existence of the group, Birdwood asked him, 'Do you know who I am?'

The sentry replied, 'Nah, and I don't want to.'

To the amazement of the staff officers Birdwood ignored the insult and asked politely, 'Been in France long?'

The sentry replied, 'Too bloody long.'

When the commander of the AIF introduced himself by saying, 'Well, I'm General Birdwood,' the Australian immediately changed his attitude.

'Well, go on!' he said, surprised and delighted, 'Well, I've heard of you, shake hands!'

To the bewilderment of the inspection party, and to his eternal credit, General Birdwood shook the man's hand heartily and moved on.

THE FIRST DAY

WILLIAM BIRDWOOD

This account comes from Birdwood's autobiography, Khaki and Gown

At 3.30 a.m. the battleships hove to, and the tows went ahead. It was very dark, and the tows got a mile or so farther north than had been intended; and some tows crossed one another. The enemy, entrenched on the shore to the number of about 900, with machine-guns, did not suspect our approach till we were quite close, when they opened heavy fire on the boats and inflicted many casualties.

Meanwhile, as soon as this advance guard of 1500 had started off, the remainder of the covering force trans-shipped from their transports into eight destroyers; these followed closely, until the men were taken off by returning tows. All this worked entirely 'according to plan'. The boy midshipmen in command of small boats earned, and ever afterwards retained, the deep admiration of all my Anzac men.

Hardly waiting for the keels to touch the shore, men leaped into the water and raced ashore, dashing straight with the bayonet upon the Turks and driving them through the thick undergrowth.

This landing farther north than was intended naturally caused some temporary difficulties; for these I must take the blame, for they were caused by my insistence on landing before daylight. But the error brought great compensations also. The original spot chosen for the landing was on fairly open ground not far from Gaba Tepe, and troops landing there must have suffered heavily from machine–gun and other fire from the trenches in that locality, which had clearly been dug and wired in anticipation of an attack thereabouts. But though, by this accident, our right avoided this danger, our left came in for bad trouble farther north, beyond Ari Burnu.

On the open beach near the fishermen's huts we suffered heavy losses; some boats drifted off full of dead with no one in control. The centre landing, in the neighbourhood of what was later known as Anzac Cove, was more fortunate. The country here was very broken and difficult, and the Turks had evidently not expected an attack, for they were only lightly entrenched and were soon driven off by the impetuous Australians.

But the crossing of the tows in the dark was to cause great confusion and, for a time, dismay. Battalions had got hopelessly mixed up, and for a considerable time it was impossible to sort them out. My extreme right was being badly enfiladed by machine-guns from Gaba Tepe, till the *Bacchante* (Captain Boyle) steamed right in, almost putting her bows on shore, and poured in welcome broadsides which silenced the enemy there—a gallant deed which the Australians never forgot.

Gradually the Turks were driven back through this very difficult country, which is covered with high scrub and in places quite precipitous. The day was very hot, and no water was available. It was a wonderful feat, therefore, that the Australians had performed—and they were nearly all young soldiers receiving their baptism of fire. Thanks to the first-rate naval arrangements, Bridges' entire Division (less guns) of 12,000 men was ashore by 10 a.m., and Godley's Division followed later.

As soon as I could, I went ashore to see the progress made, and clambered around as much as possible of the front line on the heights. Owing to the thick scrub I could see very little, but from a point later known as Walker's Top I got a fairly good idea of the situation, realising for the first time that a large valley separated the New Zealanders there from the Australians on a ridge to the east.

The men were naturally very exhausted after so hard a day— and inclined to be despondent, too. Small groups would tell me that they were all that was left of their respective battalions—'all the others cut up'!

On such occasions I would promptly tell them not to be damned fools: that the rest of the battalion was not far distant, having simply been separated in the tows. This always had an encouraging effect, though I must confess that I might not yet have seen 'the rest'.

Another factor, which did much to restore our men's confidence, was the landing of the two Indian Mountain Batteries (Numbers 1 and 6) for which I had so earnestly petitioned Lord Kitchener. Thanks to their great handiness and mobility we were able to get them, but no other guns, ashore on the twenty-fifth. Before their landing, the infantry were naturally perturbed by the fact that they were being continuously shelled, while no reply could be sent from our side.

The very first shot from one of our mountain guns (very hurriedly rushed up on the ridge over the landing-place) had an electrifying effect upon our troops, who felt they could now hold their own.

The first brilliant advance was now checked, for the Turks had been able to bring up guns and there was a constant hail of shrapnel all the afternoon. In the scrub it was impossible to keep men together, and many stragglers found their way down gullies to the beach. Later we found that our casualties numbered some 5000 all told: in round figures, 500 killed, 2500 wounded and 2000 missing, although many of the 'missing' came in later.

Some, I am sorry to say, had in their impetuosity, advanced so fast, and with so little regard for their supports or troops on their flanks, that they had disappeared right into the enemy's position.

The heavy rate of casualties gives some indication how bitter and unceasing the fighting had been. By the superb efforts of Colonel Neville Howse, my Director of Medical Services, the wounded were got away to the ships as fast as they could be collected.

Nevertheless, the situation ashore seemed fairly satisfactory when, in the evening, I returned to my headquarters on the *Queen* after discussing matters with Bridges and Godley. I was therefore horrified, about an hour later, to receive a message from Bridges asking me to return at once, as the position was now critical.

I went ashore again and was met by Bridges and Godley, with several of their senior officers. They told me that their men were so exhausted after all they had gone through, and so unnerved by constant shellfire after their wonderfully gallant work, that they feared a fiasco if a heavy attack should be launched against us next morning.

I was told that numbers had already dribbled back through the scrub, and the two divisional commanders urged me most strongly to make immediate arrangements for re-embarkation.

At first I refused to take any action. I argued that Turkish demoralisation was in all probability considerably greater than ours, and that in any case I would rather die there in the morning than withdraw now.

But, on thinking things over, I felt myself bound to place the position before Sir Ian Hamilton, if only because every report I had sent him so far (and these reports had been largely based on what Bridges himself had told me) had been entirely optimistic.

Sir Ian had little idea of the extent of our casualties at Anzac, though we knew that the 29th Division had suffered very badly indeed at Helles. It struck me, therefore, that, in view of the losses sustained by both forces, he might consider it advisable to abandon one landing or the other and concentrate all his strength either at Helles or at Anzac.

His reply came as an almost incredible relief to me, telling us to 'hang on and dig' as we were now through the most difficult part of the business. He also gave us the cheering news that the Australian submarine *A.E.2* had got through the narrows and torpedoed a gunship—a feat which opened up a new vista in the problem of checking Turkish reinforcements.

And so ended a day which will always stand out in my life: a day of great strain and of sharply contrasting emotions. I recall my feelings of confidence but natural anxiety as the troops entered the tows at 2.30 a.m.; my elation and pride when I knew that great numbers of troops had landed on a broad front and with less opposition than we had feared; my growing satisfaction as cheering reports of progress continued to reach me; and then, at night, the sudden cold fear of threatened disaster.

But directly I got Sir Ian's reply, which accorded so well with my own wishes, I felt a load lifted from me. I longed for the daylight, so I could get round to the troops.

SAM AND ME–POSTSCRIPT

STEELE RUDD

From Memoirs of Corporal Keeley

In the middle of the night we left Mudros for Gallipoli.

I was lying in me bunk an' listening to the throbbing of the engines an' thinking, as usual, what was to be the end of it all, when who comes along to see me, with a smile on his face, but Lieutenant Colonel Chaplain Brown-Smith. I never thought to ask him about it later, but I was pretty sure it was Sam who sent him.

He started telling me things about the big wars an' heroes of olden times an' was just beginning a yarn about something that happened on the plains of Troy, when I asked him what did he ever do with the old moke that he was riding when me an' Sam met him on the plains outside of Blackall.

Lord! I never saw anyone look so surprised. He stopped dead an' stared at me an' I had to tell him when it was, an' the very exact spot, an' the time of day, an' exactly what the old moke was like.

'Well, well, well,' he says, an' then he laughed an' got to telling me all about his experiences in the west until both of us nearly forgot that we had to get off at Gallipoli. Then he shook hands an' went up on deck where most of the soldiers was gathered, an' where the moon was shining, an' millions of stars twinkling like the eyes of angels looking down on us from Heaven.

Just after that we were all ordered on deck an' then they lowered us into the open boats with packs on our backs an' rifles in our hands. As the boats moved off Sam felt for me with his hand.

'Don't worry, Frankie,' he said, 'I'm here, old chap, we'll come through this flying.'

I didn't speak because I couldn't.

Then rifles started cracking on the land, an' bullets hummed over us an' past us like bees.

'Go like hell!' someone called.

'Take to the water!' from someone else.

An' into the water they plunged, an' I followed, up to me waist, an' Sam was dragging me along after him, an' that's about all I recall of the landing.

All that day, an' days an' days, an' weeks an' weeks, we spent digging in an' digging in. Every moment waiting to be attacked an' waiting for the order to attack. At least the others was waiting for it, I wasn't. I lived in constant an' indescribable dread of it.

Twice I was numbered among those told to stand ready to jump out, but I was never ready for a moment. Whether I could have jumped out if the order had come, God only knows.

'Sam,' I would often moan, sitting there cramped up in them damn trenches, 'this was a hell of a place to come to, a hell of a place.'

'Never mind, Frankie,' he'd say, 'we'll have these Turks walloped in no time an' be back home in Australia for Christmas.'

There was never any despondency about Sam, an' it was always 'home for Christmas'.

Then, one day about four o'clock, we suddenly got a warning. Hardly had we got a grip on our rifles an' stood to when over the parapets an' down on top of us came the Turks, shouting an' yelling. There was no time for thinking then.

'Frankie!' Sam shouted, an' then I heard nothing but oaths an' the clashing of bayonets and rifle barrels. I saw nothing but red, red, red!

God! I fought an' lunged an' struck at anything in a strange uniform an' above it all at intervals I heard Sam shouting, 'Frankie!'

An' I shouted back, 'Sam!'

I fought till I couldn't see a face or a uniform but a friendly one.

Then I called, 'Sam!' again an' again, but he didn't answer.

I tried to see the faces of the men I was walking over as I looked for him.

I found him lying across a heap of Turks an' lifting his head onto me knee I shouted, 'Water!'

When I spoke to him he just murmured, 'We won, Frankie.'

An' then his head fell back an' I put him down.

DIGGING IN

The Allied forces suffered severe casualties during the landings. The Allied naval attacks in the area had alerted the Ottoman and German commanders and they had strengthened their military defences on the peninsula. The forces that landed were never able to penetrate past the ridges that run along the centre of the peninsula, and mostly they were dug in no more than a few kilometres inland for the entre campaign.

The first day of fighting saw the Anzacs attack the heights in small disjointed groups, due to confusion caused by the landings not occurring where planned and the troops becoming separated from their officers and battalions. They had been landed in a hilly, scrubby tangle of ravines and steep sandy gullies. Yet, amid the confusion and lack of artillery support and leadership, groups of Anzacs attacked and briefly captured key points on the peaks of the range that commands the centre of the narrow peninsula.

By the afternoon of the first day, however, with no supply lines opened and insufficient organised reinforcements, the Anzacs were unable to hold the positions they had gained.

No covering artillery had been available as the British warships were busy supporting the other landings. Few field guns were landed to give artillery support, as it was feared they would be lost as the forces retreated. So the Anzacs were driven back and forced to dig in.

Over the following days they gained some territory and advanced into the gullies and hills adjacent to the beach where they gained a foothold along a line that would become the firing line they would hold and defend, with little change, for the duration of the campaign.

MAKING HEADWAY

JOSEPH BEESTON

The wounded now began to come back, and the hospital ships there were filled in a very short time. Every available transport was then utilised for the reception of casualties, and as each was filled she steamed off to the base at Alexandria.

As night came on we appeared to have a good hold of the place, and orders came for our stretcher-bearer division to land. They took with them three days' 'iron' rations, which consisted of a tin of bully beef, a bag of small biscuits, and some tea and sugar, dixies, a tent, medical comforts, and (for firewood) all the empty cases we could scrape up in the ship.

Each squad had a set of splints, and every man carried a tourniquet and two roller bandages in his pouch. Orders were issued that the men were to make the contents of their water-bottles last three days, as no water was available on shore.

The following evening the remainder of the Ambulance, less the transport, was ordered ashore. We embarked in a trawler, and steamed towards the shore in the growing dusk as far as the depth of water would allow. The night was bitterly cold, it was raining, and all felt this was real soldiering.

None of us could understand what occasioned the noise we heard at times, of something hitting the iron deck houses behind us; at last one of the men exclaimed, 'Those are bullets, sir,' so that we were having our baptism of fire. It was marvellous that no one was hit, for they were fairly frequent, and we all stood closely packed.

Finally the skipper of the trawler, Captain Hubbard, told me he did not think we could be taken off that night, and therefore intended to drop anchor. He invited Major Meikle and myself to the cabin, where the cook served out hot tea to all hands. I have drunk a considerable number of cups of tea in my time, but that mug was very, very nice.

At daylight a barge was towed out and, after placing all our equipment on board, we started for the beach. As soon as the barge grounded, we jumped out into the water (which was about waist deep) and got to dry land.

Colonel Manders was there, and directed us up a gully where we were to stay in reserve for the time being, meantime to take on looking after lightly wounded cases. One tent was pitched and dug-outs made for both men and patients, the Turks supplying shrapnel pretty freely.

Our position happened to be in the rear of a mountain battery, whose guns the Turks appeared very anxious to silence, and any shells the battery did not want came over to us. As soon as we were settled down I had time to look round. Down on the beach the 1st Casualty Clearing Station and the Ambulance of the Royal Marine Light Infantry were at work.

There were scores of casualties awaiting treatment, some of them horribly knocked about. It was my first experience of such a number of cases. In civil practice, if an accident took place in which three or four men were injured, the occurrence would be deemed out of the ordinary; but here there were almost as many hundreds, and all the flower of Australia.

It made one feel really that, in the words of General Sherman, 'War is hell', and it seemed damnable that it should be in the power of one man, even if he be the German Emperor, to decree that all these men should be mutilated or killed. The great majority were just coming into manhood with all their life before them.

The stoicism and fortitude with which they bore their pain was truly remarkable. Every one of them was cheery and optimistic; there was not a murmur; the only requests were for a cigarette or a drink of water.

One felt very proud of these Australians, each waiting his turn to be dressed without complaining. It really quite unnerved me for a time. However, it was no time to allow the sentimental side of one's nature to come uppermost.

I watched the pinnaces towing the barges in. Each pinnace belonged to a warship and was in charge of a midshipman. These boys, of all ages from fourteen to sixteen, were steering their pinnaces with supreme indifference to the shrapnel falling about, disdaining any cover and as cool as if there was no such thing as war.

I spoke to one, remarking that they were having a great time. He was a bright, chubby, sunny-faced little chap, and with a smile said: 'Isn't it beautiful, sir? When we started there were sixteen of us, and now there are only six!' This is the class of man they make officers out of in Britain's navy, and while this is so there need be no fear of the result of any encounter with the Germans.

Another boy, bringing a barge full of men ashore, directed them to lie down and take all the cover they could, he meanwhile steering the pinnace and standing quite unconcernedly with one foot on the boat's rail.

A NURSE'S STORY

Based on various accounts, letters and diaries

The wounded who could walk or be carried were taken out to the hospital ships lying off Anzac Cove. There were fifteen hospital ships operating at Gallipoli.

Over the next nine months one ship, the *Gascon*, took over 8000 sick and wounded men from the Gallipoli Peninsula to the hospitals on Imbros, Lemnos and Malta, or to Alexandria or England.

It was a few hours before the men wounded in the initial dawn assault started to make their way back to the hospital ships. The boats and barges that had been used to take them ashore were not available to bring them back until all the troops had been landed.

The ship's wards were soon full and wounded men lined the decks. The average time taken to put a man on board the ship after being wounded at Gallipoli was between nine and ten hours.

Most of the wounded had just simple field dressings, which were soaked through with blood, or none at all. Each of us had an orderly whose job was simply to cut off the field dressings and the patient's clothes so that we could start with new dressings. Each nurse had 70 to 100 patients to care for and that first day I worked from 9 a.m. till 2 a.m. the next morning.

There is certainly no honour or glory in this war as far as I can see. By the end of the first week I was in charge of five wards when on duty and had over 250 men to care for—and one orderly to help.

Every night there were two or three deaths, sometimes five or six.

There was a feeling of hopelessness on night duty. I tried to comfort men in the dim flickering lights and shut out the moans of the seriously wounded and dying. There was a real dread of what the dawn would bring and what each morning's death toll would be. Most men died from fractured skulls due to shrapnel wounds or abdominal wounds and loss of blood. It is best to not even attempt to describe the wounds caused by bullets and shrapnel—they are beyond imagining.

THE RED CROSS NURSE

TOM SKEYHILL

When you're lying in your bed, with a buzzing in your head,
And a pain across your chest that's far from nice,
She moves about the place, with a sweet angelic grace,
That makes you think the dingy ward is paradise.
She's dressed in red and grey, and she doesn't get much pay,
Yet she never seems to worry or complain.
She's Australian through and through, with a heart that's big and true,
And when she's near, the deepest wound forgets to pain.

With her hand upon your head, she remains beside your bed,
Until your worries and your pains begin to go,
Then with fingers true and light, she will bind your wounds up tight,
And when she leaves you're sleeping fast and breathing low.
When the ward is sleeping sound, she begins her nightly round,
With eyes that share your sorrows and your joys.
With a heart so full of love, she beseeches Him above
To watch and care for all her darling soldier boys.

There is something in her face, that can hold your tongue in place,
When you'd curse because your wounds refuse to heal.
But if once you get her cross, you will find out to your loss,
The velvet scabbard holds the tempered sword of steel.
When you're once again yourself, and they pull you off the shelf,
And send you back again to do the fighting trick,
You'll just grip her by the hand, with a look she'll understand.
Outside you stand and curse your wound for healing quick.

Though she hasn't got a gun and she hasn't killed a Hun,
Still she fights as hard as veterans at the front.
When the Allies start to drive and the wounded boys arrive,
It's always she who has to bear the battle's brunt.
She's a queen without a throne, and her sceptre is her own
True woman's smile and sympathy so sweet.
So when guns no longer shoot, I'll spring to the salute
Every time I pass a sister in the street.

THE ANZAC WOUNDED

ANONYMOUS

This article appeared in the Egyptian Times, *an English language newspaper, on 29 May 1915. It was written by an unknown British female correspondent, most likely a serving British officer's wife who wrote occasional articles for the ex-patriot British community.*

***

When, under the auspices of the Red Cross, I was admitted to the list of hospital visitors I must admit that my craven heart fairly failed me.

I had visions of myself attempting the role of ministering angel to most unresponsive patients, forcing my conversation upon those whose only desire was to be left to themselves. I imagined myself arousing suspicion as to the real reasons for my visits, seeing sights and maybe hearing things that would be inexpressibly painful to a susceptible nature such as I was certain of possessing.

My first visit, undertaken with many tremors, was, however, an agreeable surprise. Since then I have become so thoroughly interested in the cases all round me that I have extended my visits to various other hospitals in Cairo. Practically every afternoon in the week is occupied in one direction or other, while the hours devoted to such visits have become protracted till long after dark.

Numerically, in most of the hospitals thus visited, the Australasian patients exceed the Britishers almost in the proportion of three to one, and therein is conversation made easy; for besides being splendidly plucky, these magnificent Colonials are born talkers. They are never so happy as when exploiting the country of their birth, even at the expense of the 'old country' to whose defence they are sacrificing their lives and fortunes.

At times they do 'flap their wings' somewhat (and who indeed can blame them), but they are the most sociable, friendly souls imaginable, and their sociability and friendliness is combined with so much proven pluck and endurance that one does not know which to appreciate the most.

Life in these hospitals is necessarily deprived of luxury. The food is not over plentiful and, in many cases, is not particularly palatable. Yet it is rarely one hears a grumble, unless on the score of flies or the heat, and then it is more as an excuse for a joke. Murmurs over the pain these men are enduring are practically non-existent.

Like Peter Pan, the boy who never grew up, they treat life mostly as one great joke—we know one bed over which hangs the inscription 'The naughty boy of the family'.

It is only when one gets talking confidentially that one hears of the little details of home life, their concerns as to the fate of brothers and pals, the frightful tales of all they have seen and undergone, the horrors of war. Very little of their talk is of the actual pain they are so heroically undergoing.

'I'm all right, Miss, doing fine,' is their almost invariable reply to questions about their own condition.

'Yes, I'm going out in a few days, in a fortnight I hope to be at the front again, and getting a bit of my own back . . .'

'You see, it was like this . . .'

'How you would have laughed to hear us yell "Yalla imshi" as we rushed that hill.'

'Of course it was Hell, but you must remember we had been on that transport more or less for weeks; we were ripe for any sort of action. We would have been painting Cairo pink if we had been there, so we painted Gallipoli scarlet instead . . .'

'What, the bayonet charge? My, but it was fine, real bonza . . .'

'Lady, I want to write to Mother, but I can't let her know I am wounded and in hospital, so what had I better do?' (And then one suggests that the Alexandria postmark might sound more healthy and that a covering letter to the port might save the situation.)

'Cards? Yes, thank you ever so much; I am practically alone, and many an afternoon I've spent sitting on a log playing patience— never got it out for days on end sometimes . . .'

'What's this?' I asked one badly wounded man as, from beneath a pillow, I saw sticking out a corner of a little testament.

'Not mine,' was the disclaimer, 'for I don't seem to have much use for these things, but I picked it up on the beach, and it has the name and address of some poor English lad inside, so I am keeping it till I can get outside to send back to his family.' (The thought seemed to me to have a virtue high above any protestation I could offer.)

'Socks, Miss, why I can knit them myself a fair treat. Three purl, one plain, decrease down the back seam, etc. I got a first prize at the Arts and Craft Exhibition in India for knitting a lady's petticoat.' (And after the tedium of lying idle in bed he fell to work on a chance ball of wool as eagerly as a dog given an unexpected bone.)

Oh, they are a very cheery human crowd, these wounded men. They are extraordinarily thoughtful to their fellows, though they will scrap like fury sometimes, extraordinarily appreciative of their nursing sisters and visitors and extraordinarily content with their surroundings, even though they lack much in the way of creature comforts.

One watches the distribution of enormous hunks of bread and butter smeared with jam for tea, served on the pillow or little table or any other old place, where they are hurriedly covered over with a fragment of mosquito netting or none-too-clean towel. But few complaints are ever heard as to the quality of the fare. Frequently the hospital diet will be reinforced by dainties handed round by generous visitors and often the passage through the wards by a popular figure or a pretty child will take on the nature of a triumphal procession and be followed by a thousand words of interest and approval.

In spite of the rough association and upbringing of a number of these wounded, and the tedium and boredom of their life in hospital, their politeness and courtesy to their visitors is quite extraordinary. They will talk freely, though never rudely, and never forget to voice their thanks, and hope that the visit may be repeated. Quite a number of them are really musical, and, oh, the pleasure that is afforded them by an unexpected concert would soften the heart of many an amateur musician if he or she would only realise it.

The beds are frequently being emptied and re-occupied, for numbers of patients are being turned out day by day, to take their place in convalescent homes or to become the guests of private hospitality. Fatal cases have been, thank goodness, comparatively few in number as far as the Cairo hospitals are concerned. Many have been serious cases, but maybe seventy per cent are on the high road to recovery, and will doubtless face the music again with their hardihood undiminished.

One fears, though, that their future actions in the front line will never quite have the same spontaneity of ignorance, which served them so magnificently in their earlier exploits at Gallipoli. Those landing operations and their aftermath will live for countless generations among the thrilling incidents of the war. They formed an epic, one of the most heroic in history; please God that the troops engaged therein will never have to face their like again.

THE BEST TRIBUTE

JIM HAYNES

Perhaps the most poignant tribute to the Anzacs is the following poem, written by English popular author Edgar Wallace. He wrote it in response to reading accounts of the landings and then, a little later, seeing the wounded Anzacs being shown all the sights around London.

Wallace was the illegitimate son of an actress. He was born in 1875, adopted by a Billingsgate fish-porter and grew up in the poorer streets of London. He went on to write more than 170 books, mostly thrillers, and also many plays and countless newspaper articles.

In the late 1890s he served in the Royal West Kent Regiment and the Medical Staff Corps and, as a war correspondent in South Africa for the *Daily Mail*, sent back such negative reports of the war that General Kitchener banned him as a correspondent until World War I.

Wallace's novels featured sinister criminals and shadowy killers with numerous plot twists and secret passageways. More of his books have been made into films than any other twentieth-century writer.

At his peak he was selling five million books a year. This brought him a vast fortune, which he lost due to his extravagant lifestyle and obsessive gambling. When he died, in 1932, he was on his way to Hollywood to work on the screenplay of *King Kong*.

To my mind his tribute to the Anzacs is the best poetic tribute of them all.

ANZACS

EDGAR WALLACE

The children unborn shall acclaim
The standard the Anzacs unfurled,
When they made Australasia's fame
The wonder and pride of the world.

Some of you got a V.C.,
Some 'the Gallipoli trot',
Some had a grave by the sea,
And all of you got it damned hot,
And I see you go limping through town
In the faded old hospital blue,
And driving abroad—lying down,
And Lord! but I wish I were you!

I envy you beggars I meet,
From the dirty old hats on your head
To the rusty old boots on your feet—
I envy you living or dead.
A knighthood is fine in its way,
A peerage gives splendour and fame,
But I'd rather have tacked any day
That word to the end of my name.

I'd count it the greatest reward
That ever a man could attain;
I'd sooner be 'Anzac' than 'lord',
I'd sooner be 'Anzac' than 'thane'.
Here's a bar to the medal you'll wear,
There's a word that will glitter and glow,
And an honour a king cannot share
When you're back in the cities you know.

The children unborn shall acclaim
The standard the Anzacs unfurled,
When they made Australasia's fame
The wonder and pride of the world.

THE LIGHT HORSE WAITS

OLIVER HOGUE

Some of the Australians and New Zealanders had already got the call, but we of the Light Horse still waited at Mena Camp outside Cairo—growing more and more impatient every day.

It was the arrival of our Australian wounded back from the Dardanelles that settled it. It was a wrench to leave our horses behind—the dear old horses that we petted and loved, the horses that were a very part of us—but it had to be done.

When we saw our fellows coming back with their wounds upon them—when we heard of what they had been through—when we listened to their story of that wonderful landing on Gallipoli on 25 April, and of the wild charge they made up the frowning hill—all of us, to a man, begged to be sent to the front as infantry, but it didn't matter—we were soldiers of the King!

I saw the Red Crescent train as it steamed in loaded with the wounded, and I went to the base hospital to see and chat with the men who knew now what war was—the men who had clamoured so impatiently for so many weeks to be sent where 'the fighting' was, and then came back again to be nursed in an Egyptian hospital!

Yet they were happy. They had 'done their bit'. They smoked cigarettes and yarned about their experiences. I watched the slightly wounded ones marching from the train to the hospital— an unforgettable sight. Most of them were shot about the arms or scalp. Their uniforms had dried blood all over them, and were torn about where the field doctors had ripped off sleeves or other parts to get at the wounds.

As they marched irregularly along, one young fellow with his arm in a sling and a flesh wound in the leg limped behind and shouted out, 'Hey, you chaps, don't make it a welter!'

I visited the wounded men and chatted to one soldier of the 3rd Brigade who had landed in the first wave.

'Bah!' he exclaimed as he lit his cigarette. 'The Turks can't shoot for nuts! But the German machine-guns are the devil, and the shrapnel is no picnic!'

His arm was in a sling, and his leg was bandaged from hip to ankle. But he was cheerful as could be, as proud as Punch, and as chirpy as a gamecock. For he was one of the band of Australian heroes, wounded and back from the front. And we who listened to the deathless story of the wild charge they made could not help wishing we had shared in the glories of that fight.

'We fought them for three days after landing,' said a big bushman in the 2nd Brigade, 'and they made about a dozen counter-attacks. But when we had a chance of sitting down and letting them charge us it was dead easy—just like money from home. They never got near enough to sample the bayonets again. But on the twenty-seventh they tried to get all over us. They let the artillery work overtime, and we suffered a bit from the shrapnel. The noise was deafening. Suddenly it ceased, and a new Turkish division was launched at us. This was just before breakfast.

'There is no doubt about the bravery of the Turks. But we were comfortably entrenched, and it was their turn to advance in the open. We pumped lead into them till our rifles were too hot to hold. Time and again they came on, and each time we sent them about their business. At three o'clock we got tired of slaughtering them that way, so we left our little home in the trench and went after them again with the bayonet.'

'Say, what do you think of "Big Lizzie?"' asked another Cornstalk.

It is necessary to explain that this was the affectionate way our fellows alluded to the super-Dreadnought *Queen Elizabeth*. The soldier continued: 'All the while our transports were landing, "Big Lizzie" just glided up and down like an old hen watching her chickens. Every now and then Turkish destroyers from Nagara tried to cut in and smash up the transports. But the moment "Lizzie" got a move on they skedaddled. One ship was just a bit slow. Didn't know that "Big Liz" could hit ten miles off. Shell landed fair amidships, and it was "good-night nurse".'

One of the 9th Battalion (Queenslanders, under Colonel Lee) chipped in here, 'Ever tried wading through barbed wire and water with maxims zipping all round you?'

This pertinent question explained the severe losses of the 3rd Brigade. The landing was effected simultaneously at several points on the peninsula, but one spot was a hornet's nest and they started to sting when the Australians reached the beach. A couple of boats were upset and several sailors killed. Others dashing into the shallow water were caught in the barbed wire.

'My legs are tattooed prettier than a picture,' added the Queenslander, 'and I've a bit of shrapnel shell here for a keepsake, somewhere under my shoulder.'

'Fancy 10,000 miles and eight months' training all for nix,' said a disgusted Corporal. 'Landed at 4 a.m. Shot at three seconds past four. Back on the boat at 5 a.m.'

And so on.

To have gone through all they had gone through, and then to treat it all so lightly, seemed an extraordinary thing. All the doctors and nurses commented on the amazing fortitude and cheerfulness of the Australian wounded. I used to think the desire to be in the thick of things, that I had so often heard expressed, was make-believe, but I know better now.

I used to say myself that I 'wanted to be there' (and *sotto voce* I used to add 'I don't think'); and now, in my heart-searchings, I began to wonder if I didn't really mean it, after all.

I used to strike an attitude and quote 'One crowded hour of glorious life is worth an age without a name', whilst all the time I felt in my heart that I would prefer a crowded age of inglorious life to an hour of fame. Now I began to wonder whether in my heart's core, in my very heart of hearts, I did not agree with the poet. The proper study of mankind is Oneself. And what was I doing there, anyway?

Yes, it was extraordinary—not a doubt of it. Doctors and nurses said they never saw anything like it in the world. Those soldiers back from the Dardanelles, many of them sorely wounded, were laughing and joking all day, chatting cheerfully about their terrible experiences, and itching to get back again.

'Nurse,' said one of them with a shattered leg, as he raised himself with difficulty, 'will you write a little note for me?'

She came over and sat on the side of the bed, paper and pencil in hand.

'"My dear Mother and Father, I hope this letter finds you as well as it leaves me at present." How's that for a beginning, nurse?' he said with a smile.

I heard of another man who sent a letter from the Dardanelles. It ran: 'Dear Aunt, This war is a fair cow. Your affectionate nephew.'

Just that, and nothing more. The Censor, I have no doubt, would think it a pity to cut anything out of it.

I heard of another, and at the risk of an intrusion into the private affairs of any of our soldiers, I make bold to give it. It was just this: 'My darling Helen, I would rather be spending the evening with you than with two dead Turks in this trench. Still it might be worse, I suppose.'

Those cheerful Australians!

Can you wonder that the Light Horse wanted to get a move on and make a start for the front? Can you wonder that when we heard of the terrible list of casualties which were the price of victory, and when we saw our men coming back, many of them old friends, with their battle scars upon them, we fretted and fumed impatiently?

We had a church parade, and the chaplain, Captain Keith Miller, preached from the text, 'Let us run with patience the race that is set before us,' and it only made us angry. There was only one text that appealed to us, and that was, 'How long, O Lord, how long?'

We could stand it no longer. Our boys needed reinforcements, and that was all we cared about. They must have reinforcements.

It would be some days before men could arrive from England and France. Sir Ian Hamilton wanted men to push home the attack and ensure the victory.

We knew that no cavalry could go for a couple of weeks, and our fellows were just 'spoiling for a fight'. They were sick and tired of the endless waiting, with wild rumours of moving every second day. Men from all the troops and squadrons went to their officers and volunteered to go as infantry, if only they could go at once. B Squadron, 6th Regiment, volunteered *en masse*.

Colonel Ryrie, accurately gauging the temper of the men, summoned the regimental commanders, Lieutenant Colonel Cox, Lieutenant Colonel Harris and Lieutenant Colonel Arnott. What happened at this little Council of War we don't know. But we guess. Word was sent on to the General that the whole Brigade would leave for the front within an hour, on foot if necessary.

A similar offer had just been made by the 1st Light Horse Brigade (Colonel Chauvel) and the 1st Brigade of New Zealand Mounted Rifles.

What it cost these gallant horsemen to volunteer and leave their horses behind only horsemen can guess. Colonel Ryrie's Brigade was said to be the best-horsed Brigade in Egypt. Scores of men had brought their own horses. After eight months of soldiering we were deeply attached to our chargers.

Fighting on foot was not our forte. We were far more at home in the saddle. But Colonel Ryrie expressed the dominant thought of the men when he said, 'My Brigade are mostly bushmen, and they never expected to go gravel-crushing, but if necessary the whole Brigade will start tomorrow on foot, even if we have to tramp the whole way from Constantinople to Berlin.'

***

There came a day when there was sudden movement in the camp.

General Birdwood had arrived back from Gallipoli, with a wonderful string of medals and decorations, and there were other 'signs of the zodiac' pointing to our early departure.

When at last Colonel Ryrie announced to us of the 2nd Light Horse that we were to make ready, you could have heard the cheering miles away. The residents of Ma'adi, when they heard it, thought peace had been declared!

Men who had of late been swearing at the heat and dust and the flies and the desert suddenly became jovial again. At dinner they passed the joke along, sang songs, and cheered everybody, from Kitchener to Andy Fisher, and the brigadier down to the cooks and the trumpeters.

So we are off at last, after weary months of waiting—on foot. Blistered heels and trenches ahead; but it's better than sticking here in the desert doing nothing.

OWNERLESS

JOHN O'BRIEN

He comes when the gullies are wrapped in the gloaming
    And limelights are trained on the tops of the gums,
To stand at the sliprails, awaiting the homing
    Of one who marched off to the beat of the drums.

So handsome he looked in the putties and khaki,
    Light-hearted he went like a youngster to play;
But why comes he never to speak to his Darkie,
    Around at the rails at the close of the day?

And why have the neighbours foregathered so gently,
    Their horses a-doze at the fence in a row?
And what are they talkin' of, softly, intently?
    And why are the women-folk lingering so?

One hand, soft and small, that so often caressed him,
    Was trembling just now as it fondled his head;
But what was that trickling warm drop that distressed him?
    And what were those heart-broken words that she said?

Ne'er brighter the paddocks that bushmen remember
    The green and the gold and the pink have displayed,
When Spring weaves a wreath for the brows of September,
    Enrobed like a queen, and a-blush like a maid.

The gums are a-shoot and the wattles a-cluster,
    The cattle are roaming the ranges astray;
But why are they late with the hunt and the muster?
    And why is the black horse unsaddled to-day?

Hard by at the station the training commences,
    In circles they're schooling the hacks for the shows;
The high-mettled hunters are sent at the fences,
    And satins and dapples the brushes disclose.

Sound-winded and fit and quite ready is Darkie,
    Impatient to strip for the sprint and the flight;
But what can be keeping the rider in khaki?
    And why does the silence hang heavy to-night?

Ah, surely he'll come, when the waiting is ended,
    To fly the stiff fences and take him in hand,
Blue-ribboned once more, and three-quarters extended,
    Hard-held for the cheers from the fence and the stand.

Still there on the cross-beam the saddle hangs idle.
    The cobweb around the loose stirrup is spun;
The rust's on the spurs, and the dust on the bridle,
    And gathering mould on the badges he won.

We'll take the old horse to the paddocks tomorrow,
    Where grasses are waving breast-high on the plain;
And there with the clean-skins we'll turn him in sorrow
    And muster him never, ah, never, again.

The bush bird will sing when the shadows are creeping
    A sweet plaintive note, soft and clear as a bell's—
Oh, would it might ring where the bush boy is sleeping,
    And colour his dreams by the far Dardanelles.

THE MAY
OFFENSIVE

The geography of the Gallipoli region and the limited size of supporting forces available prevented the Allied troops from advancing beyond the positions they originally commanded both at Anzac and Helles.

The landings at the much better defended beaches at Helles resulted in heavy casualties and the British foothold there consisted of an area stretching approximately 8 kilometres from the toe of the peninsula to the foot of a range of hills called Achi Baba, at a point where the peninsula is also about 8 kilometres wide.

Efforts to take the hilltops failed time and again and many lives were wasted. Over 19,000 Allied troops were killed or wounded in these attempts. Some Anzacs were sent to bolster the forces at Helles, including the 2nd Australian Brigade and the New Zealand Brigade. They took part in the second battle of Krithia, which consisted of charges across open ground into machine-gun-defended territory. These attacks were ordered on three successive days: 6, 7 and 8 May 1915. The 2nd Australian brigade lost 1000 dead and wounded at Krithia, one third of its strength.

The Anzacs suffered terrible losses at Krithia. It was here that Tom Skeyhill, whose verse appears throughout this collection, was blinded.

There is a photograph of some twenty-seven men who were all that were left standing of a brigade of more than 700 after the Battle of Krithia. The hill was never taken and the campaign at Helles ground to a stalemate until forces were finally evacuated in January 1916. Those British soldiers were the last Allied troops to leave the peninsula. The battle-hardened 29th Division of the British army fought bravely at Helles and more than half their number were killed or wounded.

Having consolidated their hold on the narrow strip of beaches and hills at Anzac Cove, the Australian and New Zealand troops settled down to what essentially was a siege. The Ottoman forces controlled the heights and the key artillery positions on the southern shore. From the sea the British naval guns provided cover and protection for the Allied forces located on the northern side of the peninsula.

The infantry on both sides were entrenched along a front stretching approximately 5 kilometres and curving in an arc from near Hell Spit up into the ranges and back down to North Beach. The distance between the Anzac and Ottoman trenches varied from several hundred metres to just a few metres apart.

After the initial consolidation and digging in, the situation was stable for almost a month. Then, in mid-May, the Ottoman forces launched a fierce series of counter-attacks. On the night of 19 May, 40,000 Ottoman troops were thrown at the Anzac front line, which was made up of 12,000 men.

THE BATTLE OF QUINN'S POST

E.C. BULEY

General Liman von Sanders declared he would drive the Australasians off the face of the Gallipoli Peninsula into the sea. The result of his attempt was a slaughter of Turks that has not been equalled in the Dardanelles fighting. If any boasting is to be done, the proper time is after the event.

At least 30,000 Turks took part in that frontal attack, and on a conservative estimate, one-third of them were put out of action. The wounded were sent back to Constantinople literally by the thousands, and the sight of them spread panic and dismay far and wide through that city.

The preparations made by von Sanders for his great attack upon the Australasians were long and elaborate. For days beforehand he was busy organising the transport of great stores of ammunition to the neighbourhood of Maidos, a town on the neck of the peninsula, opposite Gaba Tepe. Five fresh regiments were brought from Constantinople to stiffen the attacking force; they were chosen from the very 'elite' of the Turkish army. He also detached heavy reinforcement from the main body of defenders, who were holding back the Allies at Achi Baba. He was determined to do the thing very thoroughly.

The attack was launched on 18 May, with von Sanders himself in charge of the operations. Shortly before midnight all the batteries concealed in the hills around set up a hideous din, swollen by the roar of the machine-guns, and the cracking of countless rifles. In the shelling, twelve-inch guns, nine-inch guns, and huge howitzers were employed, as well as artillery of smaller calibre.

Naturally every Australian and New Zealander was on the lookout; and word was sent to every post to be prepared for the frontal attack it was assumed would follow. The assumption was a correct one; for soon countless Turks poured over the ridges and made for the centre of the Australasian line.

This line is a rough semi-circle. The left, or northern wing, is on high ground where Walker's Ridge, named after Brigadier General Walker, faces north-east. To the right is Pope's Hill and then the great central gully or valley, first known as Shrapnel Valley by the Australian soldiers, but now called Monash Gully, after General Monash. Then the line continues south in an arc past Lone Pine and back down to the beach opposite Gaba Tepe.

The Turkish trenches, which are some 250 yards distant at the extreme left and right of the line, continue to get closer to those of the Australasians in the middle of the semi-circle. At Quinn's Post, named after a gallant Major from Queensland who died fighting there, the lines are less than twenty yards apart.

The trenches at Quinn's Post, right in the middle of the Australasian semi-circle and just to the right of Monash Gully, faced Dead Man's Ridge and it was here that the Turks attacked in huge numbers.

AN ENGAGEMENT IN MAY– PART 1

E.F. HANMAN

About two o'clock one afternoon the foe opened fire on us again. By now, we knew his music only too well, but, thanks to our trenches, which we were ever improving, none of us were hit. We simply crouched well down, awaiting a happier mood.

Two or three times the enemy could be seen advancing in numbers. Our machine-gun, and several others along the line, was a continual source of nuisance to them. They evidently spotted where ours was concealed, for the gunner put his hand to his head and slid gently down to the bottom of the trench. We placed him up behind us and left him until a burial party should make his last bed.

Shell after shell whizzed close to us. They were not shrapnel, but small high explosive missiles. One of them hit the machine-gun square, knocked the gun section off their feet, took the parapet clean away, and continued on its way. Strange to relate, it did not explode. The men who had been taken off their feet jumped up, laughing boisterously. They thoroughly enjoyed the fun, and as they were in no way injured, the affair was a huge joke. A new gun was quickly mounted, and as quickly in action.

The afternoon dragged slowly away, the shells were still screaming and hissing overhead, but we had become callous. Let them shoot away at us as much as they desired!

We were not very hungry, though we had not eaten a meal for two whole days, but our officer advised us to make the most of our time and take something to eat, as we might not now be feeling hungry, but we should become faint later on and unable to continue our duties, if we did not do as he asked us. So we opened beef tins and jam tins, and set to work on our ample supply of biscuits. More water was smuggled up to us, so we were perfectly content with our lot.

The sun shone down, bright and hot. We were very sleepy, but it was impossible to think of that, as every man might be required at a moment's notice. We did think that perhaps we might be able to snatch a wink at night, but we little knew what was before us Tuesday evening.

***

Stationed at Quinn's Post was the 4th Infantry Brigade, which comprised the bulk of the 2nd Australian Contingent. They had landed in early May and were commanded by General Monash. These men were put to the supreme test early on the morning of 19 May. (E.C. Buley)

***

Darkness visited the earth, accompanied by rain. By this time we presented a sorry picture. Knees and elbows were worn through. We were covered with dust; it was down our necks, in our hair, in our ears. We were all unshaven and unwashed. The rain fell gently and lightly, turning the caked dust and dirt on us into slimy mud. It was all we could manage to keep our weapons in good working order. The mud clogged in the rifle bolts and prevented them from sliding freely.

We were dog-tired. How sleepy we were, no one would ever realise! Our heads ached and swam—our senses were dulled. It was a horrible nightmare. Nothing seemed real. As we gazed with heavy stupid eyes in front of us, the earth seemed to swim around us. We found our heads nodding, and as we were just on the point of falling to the ground, our senses would reassert themselves with a sickening, sudden jar.

This was awful; it could not last, if something did not happen to excite us and keep us at fever heat. We longed for the Turks to attack. Let us charge! Let them charge! Anything would be preferable to this state of affairs!

Of course, sentries were posted, and they stood the picture of forlorn desolation, the folds of their overcoats wrapped round their rifles to protect them from the cold, drizzling rain. Their uniforms were stained a red patchy colour where they had been in contact with the slimy sodden soil. Boots were wet, feet became numb and frozen, ears tingled, teeth chattered, and we stood and shivered, thinking of soft pillows and warm dry beds.

And all the while, the rain trickled down, augmenting our abject misery. Oh! For something to happen!

What was that?

To our right front, a bright light bursts into view. What is it?

Dim figures, jet black and weird, could be seen flitting about and around the lurid red flame. Evidently, it was some sort of a signalling apparatus the enemy was employing. It looked a very clumsy affair. The machine-gunners chuckled and turned their gun in that direction. It was laughable to see that light disappear so quickly, and cries of 'Allah! Allah!' reached our ears.

***

Heavy bombardment from Hill 700, and from the top of the ridge where enemy artillery and machine-guns were concentrated, kept Australian heads down. Then the Turks dashed bravely through the scrub, heedless of the field guns and howitzers of the Australians, which were concentrated on them with deadly effect. (E.C. Buley)

***

We were wide awake now. Surely an attack was meditated. Yes! The enemy was advancing in mass formation. Our fellows had received orders to allow the Turks to come within ten paces, and then to pour the lead into them. Our rifles hold eleven cartridges, and are, in every way, very formidable little weapons.

'Allah! Allah! Allah!'

They are coming with leaps and bounds, their dismal, howling cry rending the night. Closer and closer, they are almost upon us! 'Fire!' yells an officer.

We comply willingly; rifles crack and rattle all down our line, the high-pitched music of machine-guns being audible above the din.

What a withering hail of lead met those dusky warriors. They hesitate, rally, and then, throwing courage to the winds, they turned and fled, trampling under foot their dead and dying. The air is filled with moans and cries. 'Allah! Allah! Allah!'

A bugle sounds a long-drawn, dreary note. They are coming again. 'Allah! Allah! Allah!' We can easily distinguish their officers' voices, haranguing them, encouraging.

With a very determined rush, they come again. The darkness is illuminated by thousands of tiny spitting flashes—the rattle and roar is terrific. Our dark-hued foe melts before our well-directed fire. They stagger, stumble and fall like so many skittles. Then, again, they eventually turn and flee, as if possessed.

Again, and again, they came at us, determined to dishearten and dislodge us. We had come to stay. Undaunted, the wounded were removed, all the while under a veritable rain of shot. We turned to face them once more.

VON SANDERS' MISTAKE

E.C. BULEY

Many Turks got right up to the edge of the trenches, and were shot down at point-blank range, yet still they came out of their cover, massing in every thicket and advancing under pressure of those behind.

The first light of early morning revealed to the waiting Australians a dense mass of the enemy, exposed and within easy range. Then the Australian rifles rang out, and as fast as each man could pull the trigger, a Turk fell under that deadly fusillade. Yet, still they poured over the ridges, their officers driving them on from behind with loaded revolvers, as the slaughter went on.

It was discriminate slaughter, for each Australian, before he fired, marked his man and made sure of him. It was no time for sentimental considerations of mercy. Besides, the Australians were fierce with the anger of men who had been sniped at for three weeks and had seen their mates fall as they drove on in the face of shrapnel and machine-gun fire.

Now it was their turn, and they fired until the barrels of their rifles were too hot to be touched. 'It was like killing rabbits with a stick,' said one soldier, who was in the hottest part of the fray.

All along the line from Quinn's Post to Courtney's Post the dead were piled in heaps; and still they came on. Some died grasping the barbed wire protections in front of the trenches, others fell dead into the trenches, stopped only by a bullet they met on the parapet.

From daylight till ten o'clock that morning the bombardment and frontal attack continued; then, just after ten, the Turks fell back, and as they did so a heavy shrapnel bombardment began.

The Turks sheltered for hours in their trenches while the heavy cannonade continued. In the middle of the afternoon their officers made another attempt to drive them forward, but it was a half-hearted response that was elicited. Once more they faced that deadly accurate rifle fire of the men from the south, and before it their resolve crumpled and they fled again for shelter.

All night there was incessant fire from the enemy trenches, but in the morning it died away into nothingness. General Liman von Sanders had made the most expensive mistake yet made on the peninsula of Gallipoli.

AN ENGAGEMENT IN MAY– PART 2

E.F. HANMAN

The Turk wearied first. He gave up the attempt as hopeless that night. He had learnt a lesson. The scrubby hills were littered with dark huddled forms. The cries and groans of the terrified wounded wretches were appalling. We, too, had not escaped unscathed. There were many sad vacancies. We had witnessed our comrades' heads severed from their bodies, huge gaping wounds had appeared about our pals' limbs. They had been dragged away, cursing and crying to be allowed to remain to deal sudden death to the oncoming wave of Turks.

Others, too badly hurt for speech, were limp and inert, lying white and blood-stained, clawing at the ground. Others writhed in their death agony, calling upon us in piteous tones to shoot them and put an end to their sufferings. The din of battle never diminished. Oaths and curses could be heard on all sides. Faces and figures stood out distinct and red, red, like labouring demons, habitants of the lower regions. They disappeared and reappeared as the rifles flashed and flickered.

The enemy thought to trick us. They tried to blow our charge, thinking thus to draw us from our lair. We knew, though, that we had no bugles with us. All our orders were given by whistle. They played every call they knew—some of them we could not distinguish at all, but when the strains of 'Cook-house door' went echoing through the hills, we all roared with laughter. It was too ludicrous! 'Cook-house door'! In the midst of all this butchering and slaughter! It is not necessary to relate that this ruse was not successful.

At last we could breathe, at last we could with safety throw ourselves down and rest, even though sleep was not allowed us. In fact, we no longer wished to sleep; we were too busy discussing the result of the attacks. Dawn found us still watching and waiting. How bitterly cold it was! A fierce, piercing wind was blowing, the icy-cold rain had penetrated our clothing, and we were wet through.

It was rumoured that we were to be relieved shortly. We became, all at once, jubilant and delighted. We had glorious visions of hot coffee and steaming stew. What a blessing would be a warm, dry shirt, and a good wash!

The relieving party crawled up without being perceived by the enemy. The morning was dull, and the light bad, so this was no wonderful feat. Out we scrambled, stiff and stumbling from being so many hours in awkward positions.

We made our way as quickly as circumstances permitted, past our reserve trenches. Here we saw lines of grinning, joking men, asking us what we thought of the night's attack. Snipers were exceptionally busy. Little spurts of mud close at our feet warned us that we had better hurry. Down the ranges we went, taking flying leaps, being torn by brambles, tripping and falling over stumps and holes in the half-light.

'Crack, crack, crack!'

'Run for it, boys! Come on!'

Round bends, over ridges, through slimy puddles, we kept to our mad pace. The beach presented a very inviting appearance. There were hundreds of men, all war-worn and battered, muffled up to their eyes in coats and scarves, sitting round little smokeless fires, cooking hot sizzling rashers of bacon. Its smell was to us famished chaps, simply heavenly. Then we felt safe, we had a respite. It did not take us long to make up more fires and do likewise.

How we did enjoy that early morning meal! When we had satisfied our appetites, we lay down in little groups and awaited the rising of the sun. Up he rose, bright and golden, despite the cold, damp night, it gave every promise of being a hot day.

Our hopes were fulfilled, it became very warm. The next best thing to do would be to have a wash. Here was the gently rolling ocean, water to spare, why not have a bathe? Bullets kept falling, making plopping sounds as they sent up little spouts of water. No one seemed to take any notice of these. It was well worth the risk to have a clean skin.

One of our section, who like ourselves, had come through the awful night safely, was stripped, and just in the act of diving into foam. A dull, resounding thud made us turn in his direction. We were just in time to see him reel and pitch face forward, blood issuing from his mouth. In less than a minute, we were forced to cover his face, and there he lay, a grim warning to others. There were nearly as many casualties down on the beach as in the first line of trenches.

The roll was called. We noticed the many silences as name after name remained unanswered. Every battalion was collected and drawn up in the usual manner. There were many who would never again call 'Here!' as his name was read from the roll. We said nothing, but we felt the loss of every man. Every silence was like a knife. Not till now had we realised how much our comrades were to us! We had lived with them, eaten with them, slept with them, fought with them! Now we knew their worth, now we were cognisant of the fact that they were gone. It could not be realised. Why, only yesterday, even this morning, early, we had spoken with them!

As our Company Commander listened, tears filled his eyes. He was, for several moments, unable to speak. We could see him swallowing hard, and we turned away so as not to embarrass him.

SARI BAHR

FREDERICK LOCH

If you should step it out afar
To the pebbly beach of Sari Bahr
Full many rude graves you'll find there are,
By the road the sappers drove there.

Crooked the cross, and brief the prayer,
Close they lie by the hillside bare,
Captain and private, pair by pair,
Looking back on the days they strove there.

There still they lie, their work all done,
Resting at ease in the soil well won
And listening hard for Gabriel's gun,
To spring up and salute, as behove there.

EIGHT ACRES OF DEAD BODIES

E.C. BULEY

The enemy had attacked in massive numbers, with the support of all the guns von Sanders had been able to muster. His huge store of ammunition was expended in trying to drive the Australians into the sea. But not a man budged from his post, no Turks had entered an Australian trench except dead Turks and not a yard of ground had been gained in any direction.

From Quinn's Post to Courtney's, the ground was piled with the dead and dying. 'Eight acres of dead bodies,' estimated one bushman, after close scrutiny of the field of battle through a periscope. Another tried to count the bodies in sight from his trench and stopped at an estimate of 4000.

'The Colonials were ready to meet the strain when it came,' writes one who took part in the slaughter. 'The sight of seemingly endless masses of the enemy advancing upon them might well have shaken the nerve of the already severely-tried troops. Our machine-guns and artillery mowed down the attackers in hundreds, but still the advancing wall swept on. Not till the wave was at point-blank range from the nimble trigger-fingers did it break and spend itself amongst our barbed-wire entanglements.

'Turks were shot in the act of jumping into our trenches. Corpses lay with their heads and arms hanging over our parapets. It was sickening to behold the slaughter our fire made amongst the massed battalions as they issued from concealment into the open spaces. The unfortunate Turks scrambled along towards us over piles of dead bodies.'

The Australians coolly and methodically took the chance sent them by von Sanders and every bullet was sent home in memory of comrades they had lost. They had previously displayed bravery, hardihood, and resource beyond imagination; the qualities shown at the battle of Quinn's Post were steadiness, accurate shooting, and reasoned discipline.

After being sent forward over open country against fields of barbed wire and machine-gun fire, it was a sheer luxury to lie in the trenches and let the other fellow do a bit of self-immolation.

The Australians also knew that they had struck a deadly blow at German prestige with the Turks. General Birdwood told them so when he inspected their defences after the fight was over.

TROOPER BLUEGUM

JIM HAYNES

Oliver Hogue was born and raised in Glebe, in inner Sydney. It is a sign of a different age that this inner-city dweller was an excellent horseman. He enlisted at the outbreak of war and served as an officer in the 2nd Light Horse Brigade and, later, in the famous Camel Corps in Palestine, where he attained the rank of major.

Hogue was a journalist in civilian life and an excellent writer with an eye for detail and mood. Having survived the war, he tragically died of pneumonia in England in 1919. He never returned to his beloved wife, 'Bonnie Jean', to whom he often signed his letters, 'Yours, till the end of all things.'

In 1916 Hogue, who wrote under the pseudonym of Trooper Bluegum, published a collection of his letters home. *Love Letters of an Anzac* is a beautifully written series of letters from Hogue to his wife at home in Sydney. He attempted only a thin veneer of fiction and the letters are, in effect, a wonderful series of short stories that trace the course of the campaign.

He also wrote and published another account of his experiences at Gallipoli, *Trooper Bluegum at the Dardanelles*, and stories from that collection appear in this volume as well.

MAY 19TH

OLIVER HOGUE

There is little to add about the attack on the 19th. The Turks charged all round our line from north to south. They advanced as the Germans taught them, in heavy columns, with marching tapes to keep them straight. But our rifles picked them off by scores and our machine-guns mowed them down by hundreds, while our artillery played havoc with their reserves and supports. Here and there they came in thick masses right up to our parapets, but the few who did get over were promptly bayoneted.

Time and again they charged and time and again they were hurled back, decimated and cowed. The German officers forced them out of the trenches with revolvers, but it was all futile. They advanced, yelling 'Allah, Allah,' 'Mahomet,' 'Allah,' and crawled back moaning and groaning.

Our supports sneaked right up to the firing line and offered bribes of tobacco and tins of milk to their pals just for the fun of swapping places for a few minutes. Others clamoured for a shot with exhortations, such as: 'Come down, Bill, and give us a shot. I'm a miles better shot than you are.' One chap, Sergeant Higginson, perched himself on the parapet and picked off the Turks one by one till he had twenty-nine. He wanted thirty, but it was getting very light, and the Turks started sniping again and then Higginson was killed. He never got the thirty.

Our losses were only a few hundred. It would have been far less only our chaps with characteristic carelessness got on the parapets and exposed themselves to the Turkish snipers. Next day, when General Birdwood asked one of the lads if he had shot many Turks, the soldier replied proudly, 'Miles of the cows.'

THE HOLDING OF THE LINE

TOM SKEYHILL

You have heard about the landing and our deeds of gallantry,
Of how we proved our British breed out on Gallipoli.
We charged the cruel bayonets, we faced the cannons' roar;
We flinched not from the bullets, as through the air they tore.
The storming of the hillside like the brightest stars will shine,
But the grandest feat of all of them was The Holding of the Line.

The foe, like demons, countered and the bullets poured like rain;
But our orders were to 'hold on' or be numbered with the slain.
When hot Australian temper could stand the strain no more,
We leapt out from the trenches and drove the foe before.
And now, when in Australia you hear this soldier's rhyme,
We know you'll give us credit for The Holding of the Line.

TRUCE

The Anzacs held the line against overwhelming odds, and the horrific losses on the Ottoman side led to a request for an armistice to bury the dead. This was granted on 24 May. Losses along the central area of the Anzac line were estimated as 160 Allied soldiers and more than 4000 Ottoman dead.

The first story in this section is by Frederick Sydney Loch, one of the most accomplished writers to serve at Gallipoli. A jackaroo and Gippsland grazier before the war, Loch served as an aide-de-camp to Lieutenant Colonel Johnson in the 2nd Field Artillery Brigade. He chronicled his experiences, thinly disguised, in a quite masterly novel, *The Straits Impregnable*, which he wrote under the pseudonym of 'Sydney de Loghe'. Loch appears as the central character 'Lake' in the novel.

Loch was a writer by profession after the war. A freelance journalist, he wrote several other novels, including *One Crowded Hour*. After the war Loch lived in Europe and worked with refugees for many years with his wife, the writer Joice NanKivell Loch. Their life together is chronicled in her well-known autobiography, *A Fringe of Blue*.

Here is his account of how the truce came to be part of the Anzac legend.

A FLAG OF TRUCE

FREDERICK LOCH

I had taken stand among the B Battery men, beside their periscope, where the parapet was quite low, and it needed no effort to look over the top. I fell to debating whether to take the risk and see first-hand how matters went, and while yet I stayed uncertain something happened to decide me on the moment.

There was a movement in the enemy's trench beside the largest flag, and a man climbed over the parapet and dropped down on to the open ground. He stood still a moment in uneasy fashion, next took into his hands the big white flag with the red crescent, held it overhead, and came forward.

I felt like crying out my admiration. Our snipers shot yet in scores, in hundreds maybe; and any moment a stray shot or the aimed shot of a fool might tumble him over where he stood. And no one knew the danger better than himself, for he bowed his head and upper body as does a man advancing in the teeth of a great wind, and came forward with deliberate steps, moving his wide flag in wider semi-circles. To the devil with caution, said I, and stood right up and looked across the open. 'By Jove!' I exclaimed out loud. 'By Jove!' Beside me was Mr Hay, and he looked round to know had I gone mad.

News had travelled everywhere that something special was on hand, for cries went up and down: 'Cease fire there! Cease fire!' And the firing did die away, though unwillingly, lessening and returning again in gusts, like an April wind or a woman's last word in an argument. Even when you might say the musketry had stopped, there was still a splutter and a cracking here and here, for there are ever fools who cannot help themselves.

But all this while the man of peace continued on his way, at the same stride and in the same bent attitude. Maybe before starting on the journey he had delivered his soul into Allah's safekeeping, for no shot touched him, and no quick fear turned him from the path. There was something that moved me deep down as I looked on his unhurried pace and the slow waving of his flag.

It plucked my heartstrings to see him alone there, his life not worth a smoked-out cigarette. I stood right up, all my upper body above the parapet, so that the countryside was bared before me, and a draught of evening wind born of wide spaces came a-knocking at my nostrils. All my heart cried out to him. 'My salute, friend, my salute! Do you hear me over there? It is Gunner Lake who calls. A brave man's heart is crying out to a brave man! My salute, friend! In all honour I offer my salute!'

When the man of peace had advanced halfway, the musketry fire of both sides was nearly silent, and there was a stir of uncertainty in our ranks. You heard some crying 'Cease fire' and others calling out against it, shouting there was no order, and what the devil was everyone about. But the firing did not start again, or only in short-lived bursts, and the men hung by the loopholes, waiting what might befall.

There was a stir on our side now, near Clayton's trench it seemed from here, and soon an officer came into the open, with a handkerchief tied on to a stick or rifle, I did not notice which. At the same time a couple of Turks hopped from their trenches, and another of our men went forward; and it seemed they would hold a parley then and there.

They drew near enough for me to see clearly their appearance, and it was plain they were men of different rank.

The standard-bearer was a cut-throat looking fellow with a black moustache and a complexion scarce lighter. I doubted he was a pure Turk. He was small and well shaped; but there was that in his expression which made me fear for any dog of an unbeliever who might pass his way. He was dressed in the green uniform, with their strange pleated cap on his head. Through all the dealings he spoke no word.

The man beside him, the empty-handed man, was quite otherwise. He was dressed as an officer, and proved to be a doctor. He was a man of manners, a man of civilisation, a gentleman. He came to the parley with French on his lips.

The two men crossed the half-line boundary, and came so close in that the Colonel put up his hand to stop them, lest they should arrive on top of our trench works.

The meeting was a meeting of dancing masters. They put their hands to their foreheads and bowed profoundly; they advanced and bowed once more; they smiled with utmost courtesy and bowed anew. Next they fell to talking loudly, but in the accents of men who ask the other's good health, and who rejoice at the fineness of the day. And while they talked, I picked out a seat on the mound before the parapet, and sat down to watch. It was so near evening one might sit at ease out in the sunlight.

It was a sight you might seek in vain on many a summer's day. There stood up the two great armies, the Turkish Army and the troops of Australasia, filling the mouths of the trenches, and staring one another in the face. Men that had lived days on end between two narrow, sun-baked walls, men who had lifted heads above a certain level at risk of their lives, now looked over the great bare country, and widened their lungs with breezes new from the sea.

The sky was filling with clear white clouds, the ground was sown with shadows; and endless heights and depths climbed up and tumbled away. And there were swift greens and blues and greys splashed over the picture, and earthy reds, and glistening patches of sand. And for background were the big hills leaning against the sky.

And rank after rank, from foot to skyline, stood soldiers in their thousands. The reserves were countless. Look to the right hand, and look to the left, and you were met by our men, their heads lifted over the parapets, or themselves a-top swinging their legs. And between the armies lay the debatable land, pocked with dead men and broken rifles. Ye gods! It was a sight worth the looking.

Where I sat the ground fell sharply away, and a few yards down the slope rested three of our dead, lying with heads close together. And look where you would, you would come on part of a man—a pair of boots pushed from a mound; a hand; an elbow; or maybe it was the flutter of a piece of coat. The burials had been by night—graves forced from hard ground, with few minutes to give to the building. The mounds had settled and betrayed their secrets.

Of Turks fallen in the last attack there was no end: it was a day's task to count them.

There came down the line word that General Runner parleyed with the other group. I looked across. Several men stood together, but no more could I discover.

It seemed the enemy asked for a truce for the burial of their dead.

In course of time word arrived empowering the Colonel to announce the enemy might send a staff officer by way of Gaba Tepe next morning, when the matter would be discussed.

It was all over presently. The men of truce agreed to take back the message, and fire would open again in a few minutes. Afresh they saluted, afresh they bowed: and our men came this way, and they turned that.

The Colonel gathered up glasses and periscope; and we went off to tea and the firing broke out again in a great roll.

Their staff officer rode into our lines next morning.

Certain rules were framed. Parties of so many either side were allowed over so many yards, and neither party might penetrate beyond halfway. We would take their dead to them, and they would bring our dead to us.

The day and the hour came round, and peace fell over the armies. The silence was very strange. About the middle of the morning the Colonel set off as usual for the trenches, and we started the rounds as on any other day from the B Battery observing station.

No shot was to be heard, and the trenches were emptier of men than I had seen them. Without delay we passed to C Battery on the Pimple, and there joined Colonel Irons, Major Andrews, and Major Green.

Behind C Battery and before A, the five of us climbed from the trenches on to open ground. The sun was out, but the day was cool; and it was pleasant to stand up at ease in the open. A great gathering had come about on the debatable land. It was like a day at the races, with a shabby crowd in attendance. The rule limiting the number of parties was slackly enforced, and anyone tying a white bandage to his arm to denote stretcher-bearer could go where he wanted.

In this way there were numbers exploring on their own account, exchanging mementoes with the enemy, and seeing what was to be seen. The camera fiend was at large.

PEACEABLE-LOOKING MEN

JOSEPH BEESTON

On 23 May anyone looking down the coast could see a man on Gaba Tepe waving a white flag. He was soon joined by another occupied in a like manner.

Some officers came into the Ambulance and asked for the loan of some towels; we gave them two, which were pinned together with safety pins. White flags don't form part of the equipment of Australia's army.

Seven mounted men had been observed coming down Gaba Tepe, and they were joined on the beach by our four. The upshot was that one was brought in blindfolded to General Birdwood. Shortly after, we heard it announced that a truce had been arranged for the following day in order to bury the dead.

Major Millard and I started from our right and walked up and across the battlefield. It was a stretch of country between our lines and those of the Turks, and was designated No Man's Land. At the extreme right there was a small farm; the owner's house occupied part of it, and was just as the man had left it. Our guns had knocked it about a good deal.

In close proximity was a field of wheat, in which there were scores of dead Turks. As these had been dead anything from a fortnight to three weeks their condition may be better imagined than described.

One body I saw was lying with the leg shattered. He had crawled into a depression in the ground and lay with his greatcoat rolled up for a pillow; the stains on the ground showed that he had bled to death, and it can only be conjectured how long he lay there before death relieved him of his sufferings.

Scores of the bodies were simply riddled with bullets. Midway between the trenches a line of Turkish sentries were posted. Each was in a natty blue uniform with gold braid, and top boots, and all were done 'up to the nines'. Each stood by a white flag on a pole stuck in the ground. We buried all the dead on our side of this line and they performed a similar office for those on their side.

Stretchers were used to carry the bodies, which were all placed in large trenches. The stench was awful, and many of our men wore handkerchiefs over their mouths in their endeavour to escape it. I counted 2000 dead Turks. One I judged to be an officer of rank, for the bearers carried him shoulder-high down a gully to the rear.

The ground was absolutely covered with rifles and equipment of all kinds, shell-cases and caps, and ammunition clips. The rifles were all collected and the bolts removed to prevent their being used again. Some of the Turks were lying right on our trenches, almost in some of them.

The Turkish sentries were peaceable-looking men, stolid in type and of the peasant class mostly. We fraternised with them and gave them cigarettes and tobacco.

Some Germans were there, but they viewed us with malignant eyes. When I talked to Colonel Pope about it afterwards he said the Germans were a mean lot of beggars.

'Why,' said he most indignantly, 'they came and had a look into my trenches.'

I asked, 'What did you do?'

He replied, 'Well, I had a look at theirs.'

MAY 24TH

OLIVER HOGUE

On 24 May—Queen's birthday, Empire day—we granted the Turks an armistice to bury their dead, which lay thick all along the firing line, testifying both to the vigour of the attack and the marksmanship of the Australians. Their losses were at first estimated at 6000 but we helped to bury over 3000 of them, and hundreds more must have been brought into their lines during the past six nights. Now we reckon that their casualties must have been at least 12,000.

I should mention that the Turks observed the terms of the armistice most chivalrously. Once, when a Turkish soldier picked up a grenade and ran with it to their lines, one of their officers ran after him, kicked him where a kick would do most good, took the grenade and returned it with a bow to Major Heane, who had charge of the arrangements for our side.

AMEN

FREDERICK LOCH

The burial of the dead went forward in harmony if not in love. Our fellows were good-willed enough and eager with curiosity; but among the enemy were many glum countenances. Nor do I wonder, for it is but chilly amusement gazing into the faces of your own dead.

There were many strange sights to be found in a few hundred yards' marching; but I have not time to tell a tenth of them.

At one place was a crater in the ground where a shell had burst; and round it, like chickens come to feed at a basin, lay eight dead men. It was the prettiest bit of shooting that you might wish to see. And not so very far away was a gully, maybe twenty yards long, half that wide, and half again that deep. The Turkish stretcher-bearers had gathered dead from everywhere, and tumbled them here—the place was a-choke with bodies. Hundreds were there. They lay a dozen deep. They made me catch my breath. But it was when we turned to go over to A Battery that we passed the scene it will take me longest to forget.

Four of our own fellows lay on their backs in the grass, all within a few paces. They were of those who had fallen in the first rush on the first day, and had been overlooked. Their clothes were little stained, for no rains had touched them, and their hats were still cocked to one side in the jauntiest manner.

The first man was a skeleton, picked as clean as a century of waiting might do. His skull looked out between the tunic and the hat; and through the bones of his hands grasses had woven a road. One could only gape at the fellow.

The next man waited on his back too; but the fierce suns had done otherwise with him. The flesh had decayed under the skin, while the skin had stayed, becoming a dark parchment drawn tightly over the bones. Every hair on head and hand remained. Face and hands were tiny, the face and hands of a child they were: yet the face was full of expression, and more terrible to look on than the face of any ape.

The third man was as the second.

The fourth man had swollen up and afterwards sunk down again. I had to turn away and spit.

And those four men had been filled with great foolish hopes but a few weeks before. Amen! Amen!

GLIMPSES OF ANZAC

An old friend of mine, the late Alan Murphy, gave me a copy of his grandfather's diary from Gallipoli. Alan's grandfather was Sergeant Major Thomas Murphy, a cook with the 1st Battalion, and his diary is full of extraordinarily matter-of-fact observations and comments such as:

27/5/15   Wounded at Shrapnel Gully in the head. Shrapnel shell bursts over me while taking ammunition on mules up the gully. Mules play up and I am dragged down the hillside and badly bruised.

29/6/15   Leave Anzac for rest at Imbros.

6/7/15   Return to Gallipoli on SS *El Kahira*. Cooking resumes under heavy shellfire.

7/7/15   Receive letters and news of Mother's death. Send letters home. Turkish night attack; heavy losses on their side.

31/7/15   Aeroplane drops bomb on cookhouse; food spoilt, no one hurt.

7/8/15   Captain Shout and Pte. Keyzor earn V.C. Cookhouse shelled heavily. Wounded in right eye.

16/8/15   Sent to hospital ship *Rewa* in barge . . . supplied with cocoa and food. Sleep on deck. Bullets fall on deck; shift bed to port side and go to bed.

I am in awe of Sergeant Major Murphy (who was actually permanently blinded in one eye that day, 7 August 1915), although Alan always said he was a 'cranky old bugger' in later life.

MY LITTLE WET HOME IN THE TRENCH

TOM SKEYHILL

I've a Little Wet Home in the Trench,
Which the rain storms continually drench.
Blue sky overhead, mud and sand for a bed,
And a stone that we use for a bench.
Bully beef and hard biscuit we chew,
It seems years since we tasted a stew,
Shells crackle and scare, there's no place can compare
With My Little Wet Home in the Trench.

Our friends in the trench o'er the way
Seem to know that we've come here to stay.
They rush and they shout, but they can't get us out,
Though there's no dirty trick they won't play.
They rushed us a few nights ago,
But we don't like intruders, and so,
Some departed quite sore, others sleep evermore,
Near My Little Wet Home in the Trench.

There's a Little Wet Home in the Trench,
Which the raindrops continually drench,
There's a dead Turk close by, with his toes to the sky,
Who causes a terrible stench.
There are snipers who keep on the go,
So we all keep our heads pretty low,
But with shells dropping there, there's no place can compare,
With My Little Wet Home in the Trench.

JOSEPH BEESTON

JIM HAYNES

Joseph Beeston was born in Newcastle in 1859. The son of the traffic manager on the recently opened Newcastle to Maitland Railway, he was educated in Newcastle and then went on to study medicine in London and later attended the Dublin College of Surgeons.

Beeston practised medicine in Newcastle and became president of the NSW British Medical Association and Honorary Surgeon at Newcastle Hospital. He was also president of the Newcastle School of Arts and the Newcastle Agricultural and Horticultural Society. In 1908 he was appointed a lifetime Liberal member to the NSW Parliamentary Upper House.

He served as Honorary Captain in the Army Medical Staff Corps from 1891 and enlisted on the outbreak of war in September 1914. As Lieutenant Colonel he was Officer in Charge of the 4th Field Ambulance at Gallipoli and was made a companion of the order of St Michael and St George in 1915 and was awarded the Volunteer Officers' Decoration (V.D.), which, as he was a medical man, I am sure he found at least mildly amusing.

Beeston contracted malaria and was invalided to Wandsworth Hospital, London, and upon recovery served as Assistant Director of Medical Services to the 2nd Division.

In 1916 he returned to Australia and that same year wrote the book from which the pieces used here were taken, *Five Months at Anzac.*

Beeston saw the worst of things at Anzac Cove, yet he maintained a sense of humour and commanded the medical staff with a dignity and stoicism, which is reflected in his writing. He died in 1921.

AMBULANCE WORK

JOSEPH BEESTON

Once we had landed on 25 April and our tent was pitched in a gully near the beach casualties began to come in pretty freely, so that our tent was soon filled. We then commenced making dug-outs in the side of the gully and placing the men in these.

After a few days the Royal Marine Light Infantry Ambulance were ordered away, and we were directed to take up their position on the beach. A place for operating was prepared by putting sandbags at either end, the roof being formed by planks covered with sandbags and loose earth. Stanchions of four by four inch timber were driven into the ground, with crosspieces at a convenient height; the stretcher was placed on these, and thus an operating table was formed.

Shelves were made to hold our instruments, trays and bottles; these were all in charge of Staff Sergeant Henderson, a most capable and willing assistant. Close by a kitchen was made, and a cook kept constantly employed keeping a supply of hot water, bovril, milk and biscuits ready for the men when they came in wounded, for they had to be fed as well as medically attended to.

One never ceased admiring our men, and their cheeriness under these circumstances and their droll remarks caused us many a laugh. One man, just blown up by a shell, informed us that it was a **** of a place, 'no place to take a lady'. Another told of the mishap to his 'cobber' who picked up a bomb and blew on it to make it light: 'All at once it blew his bloody head off! Gorblime! You would have laughed!'

For lurid and perfervid language commend me to the Australian soldier. I have seen scores of them lying wounded and yet chatting one to another while waiting their turn to be dressed. Profanity oozes from him like music from a barrel organ. At the same time, he will give you his side of the situation, almost without exception in an optimistic strain, generally concluding his observation with the intimation that 'We gave them hell'.

The stretcher-bearers were a fine body of men. Prior to this campaign, the Army Medical Corps was always looked upon as a soft job. In peacetime we had to submit to all sorts of flippant remarks, and were called Linseed Lancers, Body Snatchers, and other cheery and jovial names; but, thanks to the Turks and the cordiality of their reception, the A.A.M.C. can hold up their head with any of the fighting troops. It was a common thing to hear men say, 'This beach is a hell of a place! The trenches are better than this.'

The praises of the stretcher-bearers were in all the men's mouths; enough could not be said in their favour. Owing to the impossibility of landing the transport, all the wounded had to be carried—often for a distance of a mile and a half, in a blazing sun and through shrapnel and machine-gun fire. But there was never a flinch; through it all they went, and performed their duty.

Of our Ambulance 185 men and officers landed, and when I relinquished command, forty-three remained. At one time we were losing so many bearers, that carrying during the daytime was abandoned, and orders were given that it should only be undertaken after nightfall.

On one occasion a man was being sent off to the hospital ship from our tent in the gully. He was not very bad, but he felt like being carried down. As the party went along the beach, Beachy Bill became active; one of the bearers lost his leg, the other was wounded, but the man who was being carried down got up and ran!

All the remarks I have made regarding the intrepidity and valour of the stretcher-bearers apply also to the regimental bearers. These are made up from the bandsmen. Very few people think, when they see the band leading the battalion in parade through the streets, what happens to them on active service. Here bands are not thought of; the instruments are left at the base, and the men become bearers, and carry the wounded out of the front line for the Ambulance men to care for. Many a stretcher-bearer has deserved the V.C.

One of ours told me they had reached a man severely wounded in the leg, in close proximity to his dug-out. After he had been placed on the stretcher and made comfortable, he was asked whether there was anything he would like to take with him. He pondered a bit, and then said, 'Oh! You might give me my diary—I would like to make a note of this before I forget it!'

Meantime stores of all kinds were being accumulated on the beach: stacks of biscuits, cheese and preserved beef, all of the best. One particular kind of biscuit was known as the 'forty-niner' because it had forty-nine holes in it, was believed to take forty-nine years to bake, and needed forty-nine chews to a bite. But there were also beautiful hams and preserved vegetables, and with these and a tube of Oxo a very palatable soup could be prepared.

It can be readily understood that in dealing with large bodies of men, such as ours, a considerable degree of organisation is necessary, in order to keep an account, not only of the man, but of the nature of his injury (or illness, as the case may be) and of his destination. Without method chaos would soon reign.

As each casualty came in he was examined, and dressed or operated upon as the necessity arose. Sergeant Baxter then got orders from the officer as to where the case was to be sent. A ticket was made out, containing the man's name, his regimental number, the nature of his complaint, whether morphia had been administered and the quantity, and finally his destination. All this was also recorded in our books, and returns made weekly, both to headquarters and to the base.

Cases likely to recover in a fortnight's time were sent by fleet-sweeper to Mudros; the others were embarked on the hospital ship. They were placed in barges, and towed out by a pinnace to a trawler, and by that to the hospital ship, where the cases were sorted out. When once they had left the beach, our knowledge of them ceased, and of course our responsibility.

We heard many anecdotes about our recent patients. One man arriving at a hospital ship was describing, with the usual picturesque invective, how the bullet had got into his shoulder. One of the British officers, who apparently was unacquainted with the Australian vocabulary, asked, 'What was that you said, my man?'

The reply came, 'A blightah ovah theah put a bullet in heah.'

At a later period, after the Turkish offensive in May, a new gun had come into action on our left, which the men christened 'Windy Annie'. Beachy Bill occupied the olive grove, and was on our right. Annie was getting the range of our dressing station pretty accurately, and a requisition on the Engineers evoked the information that sandbags were not available. However, the Army Service came to our rescue with some old friends, the 'forty-niner' biscuits. Three tiers of these in their boxes defied the shells just as they defied our teeth.

As sickness began to be more manifest, it became necessary to enlarge the accommodation in our gully. The hill was dug out, and the soil placed in bags with which a wall was built, the intervening portion being filled up with the remainder of the hill. By this means we were able to pitch a second tent and house more of those who were slightly ill.

It was in connection with this engineering scheme that I found the value of W.O. Cosgrove. He was possessed of a good deal of the *suaviter in modo*, and it was owing to his dextrous handling of Ordnance that we got such a fine supply of bags. This necessitated a redistribution of dug-outs, and a line of them was constructed sufficient to take a section of bearers. The men christened this 'Shrapnel Avenue'. They called my dug-out 'The Nut' because it held the 'Kernel'. I offer this with every apology. It's not my joke.

The new dug-outs were not too safe. Captain Murphy was killed there one afternoon.

SHRAPNEL

TOM SKEYHILL

I was sittin' in me dug-out and was feelin' dinkum good,
Chewin' Queensland bully beef and biscuits hard as wood.
When, 'boom!' I nearly choked meself, I spilt me bloomin' tea,
I saw about a million stars and me dug-out fell on me!

They dug me out with picks and spades, I felt an awful wreck,
By that bloomin' Turkish shrapnel I was buried to the neck,
Me mouth was full of bully beef, me eyes were full of dust,
I rose up to me bloomin' feet and shook me fist and cussed.

The Sergeant says, 'You're lucky, lad, it might have got your head,
You ought to thank your lucky stars!' I says, 'Well, strike me dead!'
It smashed me bloomin' dug-out, it buried all me kit,
Spoilt me tea and bully beef . . . I'll revenge that little bit!

I was walkin' to the water barge along the busy shore,
Listenin' to the Maxims bark and our Big Lizzie roar,
When I heard a loud explosion above me bloomin' head,
And a bloke, not ten yards distant, flopped sudden down . . .
    stone dead.

I crawled out from the debris and lay pantin' on the sand,
I cussed that Turkish shrap and every Turk upon the land.
We cussed it when it busted a yard or two outside,
We cussed it when it missed us, a hundred yards out wide.

It's always bloomin' shrapnel, wherever you may be,
Sittin' in your dug-out, or bathin' in the sea.
At Shrapnel Valley, Deadman's Gully, Courtney's Post and Quinn's,
At Pope's Hill and Johnson's Jolly . . . that deadly shrapnel spins.

I don't mind bombs and rifles, and I like a bayonet charge,
But I'm hangin' out the white flag when shrapnel is at large.
When I get back to Australia and I hear a whistlin' train,
It's the nearest pub for shelter from that shrapnel once again!

AN INTERESTING CHARACTER

JIM HAYNES

Thomas John Skeyhill was born in 1895 at Terang, Victoria. His parents were native born of Irish extraction and Tom was educated at the local state school and at St Mary's Convent School, Hamilton, leaving at fourteen to become a telegraph messenger. He was popular as a reciter and was a member of the local debating society.

He enlisted in August 1914 and landed at Anzac Cove as a signaller on 25 April 1915. On 8 May he was blinded by an exploding Turkish shell at the second battle of Krithia. He was hospitalised in Egypt and following that at the Base Hospital in Melbourne. His patriotic, stirring verse was published both in London and Australia and later in New York, and he was something of a celebrity during and immediately after the war.

Skeyhill was discharged in September 1916 and his book of verse, *Soldier Songs from Anzac* was published in December 1915 and quickly sold 20,000 copies. He toured Australia for the Red Cross, lecturing and reciting as 'the blind soldier poet'.

In 1918 he undertook a lecture tour of the USA and Teddy Roosevelt called him 'the finest soldier speaker in the world'. Appointed war lecturer for the US forces, he visited war zones and later toured the United States selling war bonds.

A new form of osteopathic treatment restored his sight in 1918 and he was commissioned by the American Affiliated League Bureau in 1920 to visit Russia and Eastern Europe. In September 1921 he toured Victoria and New South Wales as a speaker and in

1926 Ohio University gave him an honorary degree. He married the American actress Marie Adels.

Skeyhill was killed when a plane he was flying crashed near his home in Massachusetts in May 1932. He was buried with military honours.

Eight years after his death, Skeyhill's biography of American war hero Alvin York, *Sergeant York: Last of the Long Hunters*, was used as the basis of the 1941 Hollywood movie, *Sergeant York*, starring Gary Cooper.

Skeyhill's fame was fleeting however, and his volumes of verse are now mostly long forgotten, though quite a few of his verses are used throughout this collection. I discovered his poems while researching in the Mitchell Library, State Library of New South Wales.

SNIPERS AND SAPPERS

E.F. HANMAN

Much amusement is to be gained from watching the manoeuvres of men as they pass some sniper-covered spot.

These snipers were always a pest. Just when one had boiled the billy, had warmed the stew or fried some bacon, one of these gentry would, with a deadly accuracy, send billycan, fire and food skidding through space. How we cursed them. But it was no use—just when it was least expected, a bullet would spurt close to one's feet. It was wise to move.

We saw our comrades throw up their hands and roll on their faces, we saw our best pals pass away in agony. We cursed, we swore, we gnashed our teeth and took shots at the suspected hiding place of the foe. There was, too, the humorous side. One chap was hit in the thigh. He grimaced and said, 'Thank Heaven! Now I shall get a clean shirt!' We saw the last of him hobbling for the beach.

The snipers were excellent shots and extremely cunning. Several were captured, most of them having short shrift, but one was taken prisoner and photographed as a curiosity. His hands and face were painted green, his rifle was also the same colour. He was entirely covered by a bush, which was fastened to his person. This disguise was wonderful. When still, he looked like a common or garden bush. It would take a very keen pair of eyes to detect anything human about it.

The Indians excelled in finding and despatching snipers. They knew the art of concealment and stealth, and could meet the Turk with his own weapon.

After we spent some time in the firing line the next two days were spent 'resting'—that is, digging reserve trenches, tunnelling and sap making. There were innumerable fatigue parties, water to be carried, ammunition to be taken to the firing line, provisions and stores to fetch. It was work, work, work.

Once, just as a party of us were turning in for the night, crouched up in our little earthen holes, a Sergeant Major came along and called upon us to come out. It appeared that the engineers and sappers were dead beat; they required help—it didn't matter how they obtained it, or where they obtained it—they must have it. We happened to be nearest to hand, and we were accordingly sent to their assistance.

Growling and swearing, we were marched up, up those towering hills. In places it was so steep that it was necessary to ascend by means of a rope, hand over hand. The hillside was a mass of white shifting sand—there was no foothold, to lose the rope was to tumble, rolling, bouncing to the bottom below. It was a laborious climb, and we were not sorry when we found ourselves, puffing and blowing, at the top.

We were then sent off in pairs, to work in different parts of the line. The saps, which we were to continue, were a few yards in front of our firing line. It was pitch dark, and the feeling of being entirely alone grew upon one as one toiled.

The sap was only sufficiently wide to allow for the entrance of one man at a time. To enter, it was necessary to go on hands and knees, as the Turkish lines were about ten yards away, and if one so much as showed a finger, a shot would ring out and be very close to adding another wooden cross to the already great numbers at the beach cemeteries.

To keep this huddled position was very tiring, and the work was slow. Every time the pick appeared over the top of the sap, a bullet would ping past and bury itself in the loose soil thrown up, and send showers of it down on to the worker. The Turks, too, were tunnelling towards us. It was a race, a race with death. We were bent upon blowing them to perdition and they were bent upon blowing us to perdition. They were equally determined to best us. Who was going to win?

Just to add spice to matters, the Turks would roll bombs towards us. They would glide, unnoticed in the darkness, right into the sap, behind the man who was digging. The trench was too narrow to turn around; if one wished to retrace one's step it was compulsory to crawl backwards like a huge crab. Several times bombs came rolling in, the only sign they gave of their presence would be the burning smell of the fuse.

The moments before the bomb would be picked up and thrown back seemed an eternity. While one of us worked away at the sap, our comrade would amuse himself by sniping the enemy. They would do likewise.

'Rotten shot, you cows, try again!'

'Here, you shot out of your turn, it's my go now! Take that, you swine, and that!'

'Look out! A bomb—quick, quick, pitch it back.'

Bang! It had burst in mid-air, just above the Turkish trench. It was a case of the biter bit.

For many hours we sweated and toiled, alternately digging and watching. The foe could be heard plainly picking his way towards us. Thud, thud, thud. They are only a few feet from us. When we stopped working, they did also. At any moment now we could expect to meet. When we did, there would be trouble for someone. We two chaps, however, were destined not to see the final lap of the race—two others, New Zealanders, came to take our place.

We crawled back, back, back, until we were once more in the front line of trenches, then down the communication trench, out into the open. A bayonet was thrust forward under our noses.

'Where the hell do you come from?'

'Sappers, fatigue party, 15th.'

The sentry, being satisfied, let us pass, and we found ourselves under the stars, standing in the midst of a large number of recumbent figures, snoring and breathing heavily, rifles at their sides. It was the 4th Brigade, at least part of it, the colours of the

13th, 15th, and 16th were visible. We were behind the firing line, behind Quinn's Post, overlooking Shrapnel Valley.

A row of still, stiff figures caught our eye, their feet and faces were turned to the sky. Their limbs looked twisted and stiff. Over their faces had been thrown handkerchiefs and rags. They were the dead, awaiting burial that night, or on the morrow.

Others, who had been sapping, joined us and we were quite ready and willing to throw ourselves down where we stood. No sooner had our heads hit the ground than we slept. It seemed a few moments only—in reality, it was hours—when we heard the Major shouting 'Stand to!' It was dawn.

We were not required that morning, however, as the fighting was not heavy—the Turks were not attacking. The Marines, young boys, mere youths, were in the trenches, so we were at liberty to rest a little longer before we should be called upon to relieve them.

The day was hot and fierce, dug-outs were hot and sweltering. Flies were a pest and the smell of the dead was in our nostrils. We passed the morning away frying bacon and making tea. While we had a chance we took good care to take a meal, a full one, too.

At rare times like that you have a chance to think and reflect. How calm and peaceful the sea looks this afternoon! Why are we at war? What is it all for?

Musings and wonderings are brought to a sudden and violent finish. With yells and shouts, the Turks are attacking. Bombs are falling like rain on the Marines in the trenches. The smoke and stench is overpowering, explosions shake the earth. Wounded are being dragged down the communication trenches. Poor, mangled fellows, crying in delirium.

The attack seems fierce and lasting. We are all on our feet, bayonets fixed, rifles in hand, awaiting the order to rush to the rescue. The trenches are full and will hold no more of our men.

'Heavens!' The enemy is in, he is driving the overpowered, fighting Marines before him. Out pour the unfortunate boys, horror written on their faces. At the time, the General was standing conversing with the Major. Now he turns to us and in a stentorian voice calls loudly: 'Come on, 4th Brigade! Show yourselves Australians! At them, boys, at them!'

With a responding roar, we charged, up over the back of the trenches, over the sandbags, up the communication trenches, right in and upon those yelling, exulting Turks.

Their joy was short-lived. With resounding cheers, our steel meets theirs. They turn and attempt to evacuate the position. No use, our blood is up, we are mad, not one of these shall escape us. Thrust, shoot, butt, they melt away before us.

The position was re-won, was ours! We meant to hold it, to regain it; many gallant lives had been sacrificed.

The Turks were making another desperate effort to dislodge us. Their short success had encouraged them. On they came, launching bombs upon us.

The General, standing calmly and coolly, under a terrible fire, exposed to snipers, exposed to everything, directed us in low clear-toned notes. He saw our predicament, and sent word for bombs to be passed on to us.

Now we could give the foe some of his own medicine. The Turk fought desperately and bravely, but we showered him with missiles, blew him to pieces, and he fell back before our onslaught.

We had won! Hurrah! Hurrah! Hurrah!

SHRAPNEL AVENUE

JOSEPH BEESTON

Our bearers continued doing splendid work after the May offensive and right through to the August offensive. As I said, it was a long and dangerous carry from the firing line to the 'Shrapnel Avenue' ambulance station or Casualty Clearing Station on the beach and a lot of them were wounded themselves.

The miserable part of the affair was that the Casualty Clearing Station on the beach broke down and could not evacuate our wounded. This caused a blockage, and we had numbers of wounded on our hands. A blockage of a few hours can be dealt with, but when it is impossible to get cases away for forty hours the condition of the men is very miserable.

The cooks got going, and had plenty of bovril and Oxo, which we boiled up with biscuits broken small. It made a very sustaining meal, but caused thirst, which was troublesome, as it was particularly difficult to obtain water.

Shelter from the sun, too, was hard to get; the day was exceedingly hot, and there were only a few trees about. As many as could be got into the shade were put there, but we had to keep moving them round to avoid the sun. Many of the cases were desperate, but they uttered not a word of complaint. They all seemed to understand that it was not our fault that they were kept here.

As the cases were treated by us, they were taken down towards the beach and kept under cover as much as possible. At one time we had nearly 400 waiting for removal to the ship. Then came a message asking for more stretchers to be sent to the firing line, and none were to be obtained; so we just had to remove the wounded from those we had, lay them on the ground, and send the stretchers up. Thank goodness, we had plenty of morphia, and the hypodermic syringe relieved many who would otherwise have suffered great agony.

Going through the cases, I found one man who had his arm shattered and a large wound in his chest. Amputation at the shoulder-joint was the only way of saving his life. Major Clayton gave the anaesthetic, and we got him through.

Quite a number of Ghurkas and Sikhs were amongst the wounded, and they all seemed to think that it was part of the game; patience loomed large among their virtues. Turkish wounded were also on our hands, and, though they could not speak our language, still they expressed gratitude with their eyes.

One of the Turks was interrogated, first by the Turkish interpreter with no result; the Frenchman then had a go at him, and still nothing could be got out of him. After these two had finished, Captain Jefferies went over to the man and said in plain English, 'Would you like a drink of water?' 'Yes, please,' was the reply.

During one afternoon a battalion crossed the ground between us and the beach. This brought the Turkish guns into action immediately, and we got the time of our lives. The shells simply rained on us, shrapnel all the time; of course our tent was no protection as it consisted simply of canvas, and the only thing to do was to keep under the banks as much as possible.

We were jammed full of wounded in no time. Men rushing into the gully one after another, and even a company of infantry tried to take shelter there; but that, of course, could not be allowed. We had our Geneva Cross flag up, and their coming there only drew fire.

In three-quarters of an hour we put through fifty-four cases. Many bearers were hit, and several were killed. Seven of our tent division were wounded. One man reported to me that he had been sent as a reinforcement and had just arrived in Gallipoli. While he was speaking, he sank quietly down without a sound. A bullet had come over my shoulder into his heart. That was another instance of the fortune of war. Many men were hit, either before they landed or soon after, while others could go months with never a scratch.

From 2 p.m. till 7 p.m. that day we dealt with 142 cases.

This shelling lasted for an hour or more, and when it subsided a party of men arrived with a message from Divisional Headquarters. They had been instructed to remove as many of the Ambulance as were alive. Headquarters, it appears, had been watching the firing. We lost very little time in leaving, and for the night we dossed down in the scrub a mile further along the beach, where we were only exposed to the fire of spent bullets coming over the hills. Our fervent prayer was that we had said good-bye to shells.

The new position was very nice; it had been a farm—in fact the plough was still there, made of wood, no iron being used in its construction. Blackberries, olives and wild thyme grew on the place and also a kind of small melon. We did not eat any; we thought we were running enough risks already; but the cooks used the thyme to flavour the bovril, and it was a nice addition.

The 4th Field Ambulance had some ingenious craftsmen. Walkley and Betts secured two wheels left by the Signalling Corps, and on these fastened a stretcher; out of a lot of the web equipment lying about they made a set of harness; two donkeys eventuated from somewhere, and with this conveyance quite a lot of transport was done. Water rations were carried as well, and the saving to our men was great. Goodness knows, the bearers were already sufficiently worked carrying wounded.

It was while we were in this position that Warrant Officer Henderson was hit; the bullet came through the tent, through another man's arm and into Mr Henderson. He was a serious loss to the Ambulance, as since its inception he had had sole charge of everything connected with the supply of drugs and dressings, and I missed his services very much.

We were now being kept very busy and had little time for rest, numbers of cases being brought down. Our table was made of four biscuit boxes, on which were placed the stretchers. We had to be very sparing of water, as all had to be carried. The donkey conveyance was kept constantly employed. Whenever that party left we used to wonder whether they would return, for one part of the road was quite exposed to fire; but Betts and Walkley both pulled through.

Early in August, soon after Colonel Manders was killed, I was promoted to his position as Assistant Director of Medical Services, or, as it is usually written, A.D.M.S.

On this I relinquished command of the 4th Field Ambulance, and though I appreciated the honour of the promotion yet I was sorry to leave the Ambulance. We had been together so long, and through so much, and every member of it was of such sterling worth that when the order came for me to join Headquarters I must say that my joy was mingled with regret. Everyone— officers, non-commissioned officers and men—had all striven to do their level best, and had succeeded.

With one or two exceptions it was our first experience on active service, but all went through their work like veterans. General Godley, in whose Division we were, told me how pleased he was with the work of the Ambulance and how proud he was to have them in his command. The Honour list was quite sufficient to satisfy any man. We got one Distinguished Service Order, two Distinguished Conduct Medals, and sixteen 'Mentioned in Despatches'. Many more deserved recognition, but then all can't get it.

WHEN 'BEACHY' PUTS ONE OVER

LANCE CORPORAL KING

Oh, Anzac Beach is a busy place with scores of men at work,
And, though we never man a trench, we help to fight the Turk,
Carrying stores and carting shell, they 'do their bit' and they do it well.
But it's duck and scatter that the load don't matter,
Drop it, hop it, you don't want to cop it . . .
You bet it isn't clover . . .
When 'Beachy' Puts One Over.

Indian fellows with their mules, Ghurkas and Maltese,
English and Australian lads, a mixed up crowd are these.
But we've all one thought the same when 'Beachy' starts his game.
It's duck and scatter, where don't matter,
Don't be slow, keep down low, let things go,
Make a dive for cover.
When 'Beachy' Puts One Over.

We mustn't stay down long, there's whips of work to do,
Those chaps up in the firing line need food and water too.
Don't think of looking glum, matters not where you come from,
After the scatter it's a laughing matter,
It's grin, buck in and load that tin,
But again we'll play the rover
When 'Beachy' Puts One Over.

THE ANZAC LINE

H.W. DINNING

Hector Dinning's writings make a real attempt to take his readers into the world of the campaign and I find that his descriptions of the Gallipoli landscape are second to none. His observations and reflections about a war being fought in a place of such natural beauty are poignant and thought provoking. Dinning was a teacher from Brisbane and a clergyman's son. His background and classical knowledge give his writing a perspective and depth beyond the scope and focus of the campaign.

***

A grand range of chalk hills runs south behind the right flank. The low shore plain of the left flank is backed by a group of green pinnacles moving north towards the glittering salt lake of Suvla Bay. To the north the coast sweeps out to the horn of Saros Bay, a rough sheer-rising headland, southern sentinel of the great Saros cliffs.

Moving inshore to the foot of the plateau one gets an impression of smoothness that is a delusion. In close detail it is rough, small ravines and sandy gullies which both hindered and assisted the Anzac aggressors on landing.

Leaving behind the beach, with its feverish busyness, the climb to the trenches follows a well-engineered road levelled in the bed of the ravine. In the sides of the ravine the dug-outs are as thick as dwellings in a Cairo alleyway, which is saying a lot!

Beaten side-tracks branch off in all directions but the only real haven for mules and horses is the shelter of the banks of the ravine, which have been dug out at intervals into a sort of extensive stable.

It is the height of the afternoon and there is no wind stirring under the hill. The men off duty are sleeping heavily. They have flung themselves down and lie, worn out, in the thick dust and heat of their shelters where the flies swarm.

Not everyone is sleeping. Here and there a regimental office is operating in a dug-out and the typewriters are busy. They make a strange resonance with the hum of bullets above, which does not cease.

The Post Office lies in a bend of the path. This is dug in deep with sandbag bulwarks. There is no sleeping here. The khaki-clad staff stamps and sorts in their subterranean chamber, amidst a disorder of mail bags and the fumes of sealing wax. One hopes the shrapnel will spare this sanctuary.

Half a mile up, the road peters out into a rough and dusty track under the hill crest. It is heavy climbing now and one realises for the first time what a task it was scaling up here at the first charge. It is hard work on a well-beaten road. Imagine what it was like for those infantrymen, hampered with their steel-laden rifles and equipment, with the Turks raining death from the trenches above! It took them seventeen minutes' work to reach these slopes. We have been panting and scrambling for forty minutes, and we are not up yet.

Five minutes more brings us to the sentry guarding the communication trench. He sends us stooping on our way, for you dare not walk erect beyond this point. Here the bullets are not 'spent' (though 'spent' bullets can do damage enough further down).

The labour of trench-making must have been enormous. Here is a picked trench five feet deep and half as wide again as your body, cut out of soft rock, hundreds of yards of it . . . miles of it!

Fifteen minutes looping around in this manner brings us to an exit which opens out into a battery position where two guns are speaking from deep pits. In a dug-out beside the pit lies the presiding genius with his ear to a telephone. His lingo is almost unintelligible, except to the initiated, but from the observers on our flanks he is transmitting corrections and directions to his gunners.

One man is juggling shells from the rear of the pit, one is 'laying' the gun, and the rest are understrappers.

The roar of the discharge, heard from behind, is not excessive. What comes uppermost is the prolonged 'whizz' and scream of the shell.

Artillery work is at least engaging and interesting. The infantry-man aims in a direction and hopes for the best but the man at the gun watches each shot, gauges the error, and acts accordingly for the next. His is a sort of triumphal progress towards his mark.

Re-entering the trench, we creep towards our second line. There are a few scattered marksmen at work here and there along our way.

There is a kind of comfort even in the trenches. The sleeping places, hollowed out under the lee of the wall a foot from the floor, will keep a man more or less dry in the rain. There are symbols of creature comfort scattered around, blankets, newspapers, tobacco tins, eggshells, orange peel and chocolate wrappings . . . but it's harsh enough. There is little respite from the crackle of musketry, the song of the bullet and the intimate scream of the shells.

The labyrinth of trenches becomes very intricate as you approach the front line. 'Saps', communications trenches, tunnels and galleries make a maze that requires some initiation and knowledge to negotiate successfully.

In the rear lines the men off duty are resting as best they can, plagued as they are with flies, heat and dust. In general they are far too exhausted to care much, as long as they have their tobacco and a place to lie. They try to be comfortable in the squalor; some even try to cook a trifle of food at their pathetic little hole-in-the-wall fires.

The most impressive thing near the first line is the elaborateness and permanency of the trenches, dug-outs and overhead cover. Also, the impression of keenness and alertness here is in striking contrast to the easy-going aspect of the reservists in the rear lines.

The men work at frequent intervals, in pairs, one observing with the periscope, the other missing no chances with the rifle.

Two things shock you and arrest your gaze.

The first is the ghastly spectacle of our dead lying beyond the parapet. They have been there since the last charge; that was three weeks ago, and they are black and swollen. They lie in so exposed a place that they dare not be approached.

The stink is revolting; putrefying human flesh emits an odour without a parallel. An hour's inhalation was almost overpowering. One asks how our men have breathed it for three and four months. The flies swarm in hosts.

The second thing you notice is the amazing proximity of the enemy trenches. The average distance is about fifteen yards.

You may be told 'Come along here, they're a bit closer' and taken to a point at which the neutral ground is no more than five yards in width, a rifle and bayonet extended from each trench would meet across it. You will need to look furtively through a loophole to verify this. Our men can hear the Turks snoring.

One result of this uncanny proximity is that the bomb is the chief weapon of offence. To shy a bomb over five yards is an easy deed to accomplish and bomb wounds are much to be dreaded as the missile does not pierce, it shatters, and there is no choosing where you will have your wound.

Working slowly back along the line you will find you are in old Turkish trenches that have been originally constructed as to fight in the direction of the sea. When our men took them they had to immediately turn around and build a parapet on the other side.

These trenches were choked with Turkish dead and to bury them out in the open was unthinkable, so they had to be buried beneath the new inland-facing parapet or thrown into pits excavated in the trench wall. The consequence is that as you make your way along the trench floor you occasionally come into contact with a protruding boot encasing the foot of a dead Turk. We had more than one such unsavoury encounter. The odour arising from our own dead is not all with which our infantry have to contend.

War isn't fun and a good deal of drivel is spoken and written about the ennobling effects of warfare in the field. The men who have had four months of this are, for the most part, pasty-faced ghosts with their nerves on a raw edge. The troops suffer from inadequate rest that is habitually broken, an entire lack of exercise, food that is scanty and ill-nourishing, a perpetual and overpowering stink of the most revolting kind and black swarms of flies that make rest impossible even if the enemy shelling and bomb-throwing did not. Then there is the nervous strain of suspense and known peril that is never lifted.

Australians have done their part with unequalled magnificence but flesh and blood and spirit cannot go at this indefinitely. God help the Australian infantryman who has less than a frame of steel wire, muscles of whipcord and a heart of fire.

In rare cases men have been driven demented in our firing line. Men who were in civilian life modest, gentle, tender-hearted and self-effacing have become bloody minded, lusting to kill. War is not fun, neither is it ennobling.

It is by way of Shrapnel Valley that we regain the beach. The Australian hospital stands on the right extremity, by no means out of danger. A sparse line of stretchers is moving down almost continuously. This is a hospital for mere hasty dressing to enable the wounded to go aboard the pinnaces and out to the hospital ship standing offshore.

Collins Street doctors who have left behind practices replete with every convenience find themselves working in hastily erected marquees where half the attendants limp or hop.

The beach is animated. There are innumerable wireless stations, ordnance stores, medical supply stores and A.S.C. depots. Here are the hard facts and hard graft; dirt, sweat and peril of righteous war. It is by these mundane means, rather than pride, pomp and circumstance, that the clash of ideals is progressing, and by which a decision will come.

Here on the beach the morning splash has become indispens-able to some. Daily at six-thirty you see the bald pate of General Birdwood bobbing beyond the sunken barge just offshore, and a host of nudes lining the beach. As the weather cools the host is slowly diminishing to a few isolated fellows who are either fanatics or have come down from the trenches to clear up vermin and dust-infested skin at all costs.

Naturally men would prefer to bathe at midday, rather than at 6.30 a.m. when the sun has not got above the precipitous ridge of Sari Bair. But the early morning dip is almost the only safe one. The beach is still enfiladed by Turkish artillery from the right although this is better than previously when enemy guns from both flanks commanded the beach. The gun on the right somewhere that continues to harass us is known familiarly as 'Beachy Bill'. The one that was formerly active on the left went by a name intended for the ears of soldiers only.

'Beachy Bill' is, in fact, the collective name for a whole battery capable of throwing over five shells simultaneously. 'Beachy Bill' sometimes catches the morning bathing squad and then there is much ducking and splashing shoreward and scurrying over the beach to cover by men clad only in the garments nature provided.

Shrapnel bursting above the water raises the question: will it ever stop? Will the pellets ever cease to whip the water? The interval between the murderous lightning burst aloft and the last pellets whipping the water seems everlasting to the potential victim.

The hidden battery cannot be located. The cruisers are doing their best with searching fire, their blue-jackets are climbing the masts to observe, the balloon is aloft, the seaplanes are vigilant, our own artillery outposts never relax . . . but there is no clue. It is concealed with devilish ingenuity. Every day it is costing us dearly.

All's fair in war. Turkish sniping is awfully successful. The Turkish sniper is almost unequalled, certainly unexcelled, as an unerring shot. They have picked off our officers at a deadly rate. Lance Corporals have become Lieutenants in a single night.

Transport of supplies to the flanks is done by mule-carts manned by Sikhs. The route is sniped by night as well as by day and is swept by shrapnel and machine-gun fire. Only under the most urgent necessity are supplies taken to the flanks by day and then the loss in men and mules is heavier than we can rightly bear.

Sickness also has diminished little. Colic, enteric, dysentery and jaundice are still painfully prevalent and our sick are far flung and many in Lemnos, Egypt, Malta and England. As long as the flies and the unburied persist, the wastage in sick men deported is near to alarming.

Along with disease it's the monotony that kills those away from the front lines, not hard work or hard fare. We have now been embarked here for four months and there has been little change in our way of living. Every day there is the same work on the same beach, shelled by the same guns. Presumably the same guns are manned by the same Turks, for we never seem to knock out those furtive and deadly batteries that maim and kill almost daily.

MY COSY LITTLE DUG-OUT ON THE HILL

CORPORAL G.L. SMITH

Come and see my little dug-out—way upon a hill it stands
From where I get a lovely view of Anzac's golden sands;
When 'Beachy Bill' is shelling, I can see just where it lands,
From my cosy little dug-out on the hill.

Now, it isn't quite as roomy as the mansions of the Tsar,
From sitting room to bedroom really isn't very far,
For the dining and the smoking room—you stay just where
    you are,
In my cosy little dug-out on the hill.

The fleas all wander nightly, just as soon as I've undressed,
And after many weary hunts I've had to give them best.
And the ants have also found it, so there's very little rest
In my cosy little dug-out on the hill.

I've a natty little cupboard, which looks so very nice,
It was made to keep my bread and jam, my bacon and my rice;
But now it's just a comfy little home for orphaned mice,
In my cosy little dug-out on the hill.

There is no electric lighting in this blighted land of war,
So I use some fat in syrup tins, which stand upon the floor.
And when that's burning brightly, well I sweat from every pore,
In my cosy little dug-out on the hill.

When the nights are clear and starry and the scenery beautified
By the silvery gleams and shadows then I often sleep outside;
But when it's wet and stormy—well, I just crawl in and hide
In my cosy little dug-out on the hill.

When it's time for parting from my little eight by four,
I'll finally get a good night's rest without a back that's sore,
Perhaps some day I'll miss it and will long to live once more
In my cosy little dug-out on the hill.

SIDELIGHTS OF BATTLE

ANONYMOUS—AN ARTICLE IN *THE SUN*, SYDNEY 1916

'I'll never forget,' says Corporal Carnegie, 'my first feeling after killing a man. I took aim and that, all right, I fired and he fell dead. I shook all over, and felt as if I had murdered him, and then I heard myself saying to my neighbour, "There now, I've killed him, the poor beggar!" You soon get over that, though, and after a short time become as deliberate and callous as possible.

'It is marvellous how short a time war takes to change the make of you. When I arrived in Gallipoli I fancied the men I saw must be a different kind to myself. They paced up and down the trenches looking like wild beasts. You never saw anything like the look in their eyes—wild and staring. And when, after the evacuation, I got back to Cairo, the chaps who had not yet been into action remarked the same expression in my own eyes! So there you are!'

Corporal Carnegie's expression now is the mildest and cheeriest in the world. You cannot imagine that it was ever wildly staring. He, like others, found waiting for the order to charge the most nerve-racking of all war's trials.

'Five minutes to go!

'Three minutes to go!

'Over!

'And then men who have been trembling and fearful leap over the parapet with shouting and laughter.

'I saw a bit of a kid cowering in a corner when the order was given to fire. I took not a bit of notice of him, and my mate said, "All right, leave him alone; he'll be at it presently." And sure enough, in a little while the youngster got up and took his rifle. His face was white as death, but I saw him lean right over the parapet and take aim. His gun was hot before he stopped firing, and the enemies' bullets were kicking the dust up all around him.

'There was another youngster I shan't forget in a hurry. It was his first experience of bombs. One burst in the trench, and he ran just as hard as he could to the end of the sap. Yes, he came back again very ashamed of himself, until I told him, "It's all right, laddie, I've felt that way myself."

'During a bombardment you don't feel in the least excited or nervy. It's the next day, or when you try to sleep, that it gets to you. Dream? I should smile. But they generally give you rum after heavy action, so that you fall into a sound sleep without any trouble.

'I used to duck like anything when first I saw action, but it was not long before I laughed with the rest when a sniper took off the branch of a tree above my head. Funny, when you're going into the firing line you never feel it's yourself won't come back again. You are quite sure you'll get through all right, and you feel sorry for the others when you look round during the service beforehand, and consider that never again will this complete set of men stand round while the chaplain reads.

'Once at Gallipoli we saw a young Turk lying dead in the most beautiful position for firing. He was prone with his rifle sighted. Our fellows waited till night to drag him in and go through his papers. He was only nineteen, and there was a half-written letter in his pocket to his mother. It was in Arabic. In his kit bag we found a nice clean suit of pyjamas, a tin of roast beef, and clothes nicer than our own. His mother must have been fond of that kid.

'We ate the roast beef, and my word it was a treat after Gallipoli bully beef!'

THE RAGTIME ARMY

ANONYMOUS

We are the ragtime army, the A.N.Z.A.C.,
We cannot shoot, we won't salute,
What bloody good are we?
And when we get to Berlin Old Kaiser Bill says he:
'Hoch, hoch, mein Gott, what a lousy rotten lot,
Are the A.N.Z.A.C.'

NOT DEAD YET

JOSEPH BEESTON

Anzac will be a wonderful place for tourists after the war is over. For Australians particularly it will have an unbounded interest. The trenches where the men fought will be visible for a long time, and there will be trophies to be picked up for years to come. All along the flat land by the beach there are sufficient bullets to start a lead factory.

The beaches are pleasant and the water is perfect for swimming and fishing.

Our men had a novel way of fishing; they threw a bomb into the water, and the dead fish would either float and be caught or go to the bottom—in which case the water was so clear that they were easily seen. There was one fish that was common, they were something like a mackerel, and were delicious.

One thing that was really good in Anzac was the swimming. At first we used to dive off the barges; then the Engineers built Watson's Pier, at the end of which the water was fifteen feet deep and as clear as crystal, so that one could see every pebble at the bottom. At times the water was very cold, but always invigorating.

General Birdwood was an enthusiastic swimmer, but he always caused me a lot of anxiety. That pier was well covered by Beachy Bill, and one never knew when he might choose to give it his attention. This did not deter the General. He came down most regularly, sauntered out to the end, went through a lot of Sandow exercises and finally jumped in. He then swam out to a buoy moored about a quarter of a mile away. On his return he was most leisurely in drying himself. Had anything happened to him I don't know what the men would have done, for he was adored by everyone.

Swimming was popular with all hands. Early in the campaign we had a Turkish attack one morning; it was over by midday, and an hour later most of the men were in swimming.

I think it not unlikely that some of the 'missing' men were due to this habit. They would come to the beach and leave their clothes and identity discs ashore, and sometimes they were killed in the water. In this case there was no possibility of ascertaining their names. It often struck me that this might account for some whose whereabouts were unknown.

My little dog Paddy enjoyed the swim almost as much as I did. He was a great favourite with everybody but the Provost Marshal. This official was a terror for red tape, and an order came out that dogs were to be destroyed. That meant that the Military Police were after Paddy. However, I went to General Birdwood, who was very handsome about it, and gave me permission to keep the little chap. Almost immediately after he was reprieved he ran down to the Provost Marshal's dug-out and barked at him. Paddy was very nearly human.

One day we were down as usual when Beachy Bill got busy, and I had to leave the pier with only boots and a smile on. I took refuge behind my old friends the biscuits, and Paddy ran out to each shell, barking until it exploded. Finally one burst over him and a bullet perforated his abdomen. His squeals were piteous. He lived until the next day, but he got a soldier's burial.

While swimming, the opportunity was taken by a good many to soak their pants and shirt, inside which there was, very often, more than the owner himself. I saw one man fish his pants out; after examining the seams, he said to his pal, 'They're not dead yet.'

His pal replied, 'Never mind, you gave them a hell of a fright.'

These insects were a great pest, and I would counsel friends sending parcels to the soldiers to include a tin of insecticide; it was invaluable when it could be obtained.

I got a fright myself one night. A lot of things were doing the Melbourne Cup inside my blanket. The horrible thought suggested itself that I had got 'them' too, but a light revealed the presence of fleas. These were very large able-bodied animals and became our constant companions at night-time; in fact one could only get to sleep after dosing the blanket with insecticide.

LAMENT

LANCE CORPORAL SAXON

It ain't the work and it ain't the Turk
That causes us to swear,
It's having to fight at dark midnight
With the things in our underwear.

They're black and grey and brindle and white
And red and big and small
And they steeplechase around our knees
And we cannot sleep at all.

Today there's a score, tomorrow lots more
Of the rotters, it ain't too nice
To sit, skin bare in the morning air,
Looking for blooming lice!

'PRAISE GOD FROM WHOM ALL BLESSINGS FLOW'

JOSEPH BEESTON

No account of the war would be complete without some mention of the good work of the chaplains. They did their work nobly, and gave the greatest assistance to the bearers in getting the wounded down. I came into contact chiefly with those belonging to our own Brigade—Colonel Green, Colonel Wray, and Captain Gillitson, who was killed while trying to get to one of our men who had been wounded.

Services were held whenever possible, and sometimes under very peculiar circumstances.

Once a service was being conducted in the gully when a platoon was observed coming down the opposite hill in a position exposed to rifle fire. The thoughts of the audience were at once distracted from what the Padre was expounding by the risk the platoon was running; and members of the congregation pointed out the folly of such conduct, emphasising their remarks by all the adjectives in the Australian vocabulary.

Suddenly a shell burst over the platoon and killed a few men. After the wounded had been cared for, the Padre regained the attention of his congregation and gave out the last verse of 'Praise God from Whom all blessings flow'.

There was one man for whom I had a great admiration—a clergyman in civil life but a stretcher-bearer on the Peninsula— Private Greig McGregor. He belonged to the 1st Field Ambulance, and I frequently saw him. He always had a stretcher, either carrying a man or going for one, and in his odd moments he cared for the graves of those who were buried on Hell Spit. The neatness of many of them was due to his kindly thought. He gained the Distinguished Conduct Medal, and richly deserved it.

All the graves were looked after by the departed one's chum. Each was adorned with the Corps' emblems: thus the Artillery used shell caps, the Army Medical Corps a Red Cross in stone, etc.

There were very few horses on the Peninsula, and those few belonged to the Artillery. But at the time I speak of we had one attached to the New Zealand and Australian Headquarters, to be used by the despatch rider.

Anzac, the Headquarters of General Birdwood, was about two and a half miles away; and, being a true Australian, the despatch-carrier declined to walk when he could ride, so he rode every day with despatches. Part of the journey had to be made across a position open to fire from Walker's Ridge.

We used to watch for the man every day, and make bets whether he would be hit. Directly he entered the fire zone, he started as if he were riding in the Melbourne Cup, sitting low in the saddle, while the bullets kicked up dust all round him.

One day the horse returned alone, and everyone thought the man had been hit at last; but in about an hour's time he walked in. The saddle had slipped, and he came off and rolled into a sap, whence he made his way to us on foot.

When going through the trenches it is not a disadvantage to be small of stature. It is not good form to put one's head over the sandbags; the Turks invariably objected, and even entered their protest against periscopes, which are very small in size. Numbers of observers were cut about the face and a few lost their eyes through the mirror at the top being smashed by a bullet.

On one occasion I was in a trench which the men were making deeper. A rise in the bottom of the trench just enabled me, by standing on it, to peer through the loophole.

On commending the man for leaving this lump in the floor of the trench, he replied, 'That's a dead Turk, sir!'

ARCADIA

H.E. SHELL

I've dwelt in many a town and shire from Cairns to Wangaratta;
I've dropped into the Brisbane Show and Bundaberg Regatta,
But now I've struck the ideal spot where pleasure never cloys,
Just list' to the advantages this choice retreat enjoys—
The scenery is glorious, the sunsets are cyclonic;
The atmosphere's so full of iron, it acts as quite a tonic!

No parsons ever preach the Word or take up a collection;
While politicians don't exist, nor any by-election.
No scandal ever hovers here to sear our simple lives;
And married men are always true to absent, loving wives.
And should you doubt if there can be a spot which so excels,
Let me whisper—it is ANZAC! Anzac by the Dardanelles.

THE AUGUST
OFFENSIVE

The next real development in the campaign occurred in August when a new invasion was undertaken at Suvla Bay to the north of Anzac. This force of some 15,000 men was to land at Suvla on 6 August and advance across a dry salt lake and hilly open plain toward the Anafurta Range, Hill 971 and Chunuk Bair, with a view to stretching a cordon across the peninsula and crumpling up the right wing of the Turkish army.

Attacks by all forces on the peninsula were planned to divert Ottoman attention from the landing and enable this new force to become an important part of a pincer movement against the heights.

These invasion forces were all newcomers to war and were young, poorly trained and poorly led. The command was given to Sir Frederick Stopford, who had been retired since 1909, was sixty-one years old, and had never commanded men in battle.

Stopford never even went ashore. He stayed on the British sloop *Jonquil* while his invading force suffered casualties of 1700 men on shore. The number of British casualties was actually greater than the number of Turks opposing them.

Whatever the reason—unclear orders, poor morale after a botched landing, heat and difficult terrain, heavy Turkish resistance, or simply poor and hesitant leadership—the forces that landed at Suvla Bay on 6 and 7 August failed to advance as expected.

Meanwhile the Anzacs attacked according to plan. The Australians charged the Ottoman trenches at Lone Pine and captured them while the New Zealanders charged up Rhododendron Ridge and took Chunuk Bair. Due to a mis-timed artillery barrage and a failed attempt to capture the German Officers' Trench and take out the Turkish machine guns, the Light Horse Brigade, fighting as infantry, charged into the face of machine-gun fire and died at the Nek.

At Helles the 29th Division made yet another futile and tragic attack on Krithia.

The forces at Suvla Bay, however, did not advance to achieve their objective and the plan failed.

Allied losses all round were devastating. More than 2000 Australians died at Lone Pine alone. On the other side, losses were even worse; 7000 Ottoman troops died defending Lone Pine.

Ottoman troops under Mustafa Kemal recaptured the heights from the New Zealanders and Ghurkas on 10 August. The Anzacs held Lone Pine until the evacuation, and the Allies effectively held most of the Suvla Bay area and Anafurta Plains after another concerted push with reinforcements finally allowed the forces at Anzac to link up with the forces at Suvla on 27 August.

LONE PINE

WILLIAM BAYLEBRIDGE

Of all those battles fought by our troops at Anzac, none was more fierce, and few were more bloody, than that waged at Lone Pine.

Shut too long in their trenches, with little room to pass beyond them and taking death, night and day, from the shells the Turks hurled into their lines, our troops' only desire was to be out and upon the move. Not only did Australian bayonets bring it through to a right end, but such things as were done there put Australian courage forever past doubt.

Lone Pine stood against the centre of our line. It was high land and so strong was the Turks' position there, both in defence-works and men, that any soldier, skilled in his trade, would have thought it impossible to be taken at all. The Turkish front trenches were roofed in with heavy logs, which were covered up with earth. Shelling, from our guns and ships, had little effect there.

Machine-guns were set into the Turkish front line and room had been made there for snipers and for those who threw bombs out. In front of all these traps lay an ugly tangle of barbed wire. The open land further out was swept clean by rifle fire from both ends of the ridge, for the Turks controlled a dozen positions further north, and also many to the south. Turkish artillery had the accurate range of this country to a hair.

On the afternoon of the sixth day of August, a great bombardment of shellfire, from our ships behind us and our batteries on land, was poured into the wire and the Turkish back trenches at Lone Pine. These back trenches were not covered up and great numbers of Turks had been gathered there to defend that position. Those back trenches were soon choked up with dead and wounded.

While this was going on the Turkish gunners, shooting as often as they might, gave back something of what they got. With the roaring of guns, and the screech of that flying shell, there was little peace that afternoon. But then, all at once, our guns ceased firing and the charge was blown. Like hounds loosed from a leash, off raced our men: with bayonets fixed, up and over the parapet they leapt, and charged.

That charge might well have stirred the blood in any man! Those men raced toward the enemy trenches, spat upon by rifle fire from every loophole, cut down by machine-guns, torn through by a rain of shrapnel, and not one hesitated. Thick they fell but they cared not. Believe me, it was not hard, later, to see the way they had gone, so heavy-sown it was with men dead.

Thinned out, but with Australian hearts yet, those who could swept on, pushed through the twisted wire, and swarmed at last up the parapet of the Turks. Once up and on that parapet, did these Australians wait? No, they tore up the roof from those front trenches and leapt down into a darkness ripe with death.

Then was there bloody work! In and home went their steel; it had a thirst in it for the blood of those Turks. Then did they fight like the men they were, now thrusting, now holding off, now twisting, now turning, now wrenching out their bayonets from this crush of flesh, now dropping down with their limbs shattered, with their bowels slit and torn out by the foe.

Along through those trenches, dark and stinking, men fought hand to hand. Many, with clubbed rifle, spilt out the brains of others, trodden soon to mud on the floor there. Bombs, knives, whatever came next to hand, both foe and friend brought into use. The bombs, bursting in little room, did great hurt: many a press of tough men they tore up, limb away from limb, making a right sickening mess.

Here and there the Turks got together in knots so that they might better hold out; but the steel of Australia ploughed a passage through those trenches. Little then did it help those Turks to know every corner, each turn and short cut, of that place; little then did their valour help them. As the two sides fought on in the heat and choking stench of that darkness, the dead lay thick under foot, here two-deep, three-deep there, and there four-deep.

Now, you have heard how these men of Australia, that tore the roof up and off those trenches, got *their* part done. While all this was doing, there were others who took those Turks in the rear. These men had charged on over the roofed trenches and struck out for the trenches behind. Coming up to these trenches—filled now with the death our guns had dealt—they pushed in, and sealed up behind them the passages that linked the back trenches with the front lines, so that the Turks could by no means get out.

Thus, taking the foe both in front and upon the rear, our steel drove them in and back upon themselves, and slew them like sheep in some accursed shambles. Too many of our own men as well were slain there! Neither friend nor foe escaped and the trenches were choked up with dead men and dying.

So thick lay the dead that we later piled them to the height of a tall man, and had to prop them up behind logs, and hold them up out of the trench with ropes, so that one side of the passage might be kept clear. Never, surely, was there a battle fought more fiercely hand to hand!

Our men, at last, got the better of those Turks. Those still alive and stirring, we drove up out of the ground and fell upon. Some we slew fighting; some, making off as they best might through the open, we caught with our machine-guns; some we pushed up into saps where they were glad to give over.

As for their counter-attacks, the Turks made many, and in fine style; but, though these attacks cost us many good men, they cost the foe more, and were but lost labour.

Three days and three nights this battle lasted. The loss upon our side was a hard loss—we buried above 2000 slain.

As for the men who fought in this battle, all were infantry. There were men of the 1st Brigade in the first attack and, in the relief and making good the victory, men of the 2nd Brigade.

THE GLORIOUS CHARGE

OLIVER HOGUE

Talk about the Charge of the Light Brigade! Well, all I've got to say is that this war will make us readjust the estimates of old-time battles and exploits. The capture of Lone Pine was a feat of arms that the Pretorian Guard or Cromwell's Ironsides or Napoleon's Old Guard would have gloried in having to their credit. We who watched were spellbound.

The irregular khaki line charged with reckless indifference to the hail of shrapnel and rifle fire and machine-guns. A well-trained regiment of Gay Gordons or Grenadiers or Fusiliers would have charged in a beautiful line—and probably would have been mown down like wheat before the scythe. But our chaps don't fight that way. They raced forward as individuals, not as a battalion. Each man's initiative spurred him on to do deeds of valour with his own hand. But for this their casualties would have been far greater.

We saw them falter just for a second—but it was only to hack the barbed wire out of their path. Then they jumped into the trenches and slaughtered the Turks with the bayonet. Oh, Honey, it was magnificent! It was War. Once again we Light Horsemen stand and salute and do honour to our comrades of the Infantry.

When the heroic band reached the Turkish trenches they found them protected with overhead cover, pine logs and brushwood and earth, with only an opening here and there. But with magnificent daring our boys bayoneted the defenders, jumped down among the swarming Turks and plied the bayonet like demons.

Then our supporting columns, dashing across the intervening hell, overran the first line of trenches, captured the second defence, captured or bayoneted the inmates, linked up with the storming party, and Lone Pine was ours ... A hundred years hence the people of Australia will talk with bated breath of the glorious charge. Our 2nd Light Horse Brigade and the 2nd Infantry Brigade held the ridge against all the furious counter-attacks of the Turks, but it was the gallant 1sts who deserve the most of the glory.

Note: Seven Victoria Crosses were won at Lone Pine.

FALLEN COMRADES

ANONYMOUS

Halt! Thy foot is on heroes' graves;
    Australian lads lie sleeping below;
Just rough wooden crosses at their heads,
    To let their comrades know.
They'd sleep no better for marble slabs,
    Or monuments so grand;
They lie content, now their day is done,
    In that far-off Turkish land.

The wild flowers are growing o'er them,
    The white heath blooms close by;
The crickets chirp around them,
    Above, the free birds fly;
Wild poppies thrive beside them,
    Their bloom is scarlet born—
Red poppies—sleep-flowers, emblems
    Of that blood-red April morn.

The blue sea seems a-sighing,
    In the morning air so clear,
As though grieving o'er the fallen,
    Who never knew a fear.
A lonesome pine stands near-by;
    A grim sentinel it stands,
As though guarding the last resting-place
    Of that gallant little band.

I've often passed those little mounds,
    And heard the bullets meow,
When the air was full of shrapnel;
    'Tis called Shrapnel Gully now.
Whilst coming from the trenches
    And glancing over there,
I've oft seen many a khaki form,
    Kneeling in silent prayer.

Kneeling o'er fallen comrades,
    Perhaps their boyhood's chums,
Felled by the shrieking shrapnel
    Or the deadly snipers' guns.
They were only rough Australians,
    Fiends in the bayonet rush;
But there, with their fallen comrades,
    They knelt in the evening's hush.

Their backs turned to the trenches—
    The first time to the foe—
Their heads bent low in sorrow,
    Down their cheeks the salt tears flow;
Who knows what silent prayer
    Their hearts speak—who can tell?
With hands laid on the rough graves
    They say their last farewell.

The Sikh and the Punjaber,
    With their pack mules oft pass by,
And when they see those kneeling forms
    Their cheeks are not quite dry.
I've rushed back to the trenches,
    Cursing the Turkish foe,
Then, gaze on my sleeping comrades,
    Wondering who next would go.

There's many a loving mother,
    Home in Australia dear,
Who is thinking, broken-hearted,
    Of her loved son's distant bier;
There's many a true Australian girl,
    Stricken with sudden pain,
Mourning for her dead sweetheart,
    Whom she'll never see again.

They know not where he's lying,
    Or how their loved one fell;
That's why these lines are written,
    The simple truth to tell.
Their graves are on Gallipoli,
    Up in the very heights,
Above the rugged landing-place,
    Scene of the first great fights.

Shrapnel Gully is on their right,
    Courtney's Post at their head,
The Mediterranean at their feet
    And the blue sky overhead.
Their burial march was the big guns' roar,
    Their greatcoat their winding sheet,
Their head is to the firing line
    And the ocean at their feet.

Officers and privates, who fell
    In that first fierce rush of fame,
They lie there, comrade by comrade;
    Their rank is now the same.
The city boy from his ledger,
    The country boy from his plough,
They trained together in Egypt,
    And sleep together now.

Your graves may be neglected,
    But fond mem'ry will remain;
The story of how you fought and died
    Will ease the grief and pain
That we know your kin are feeling
    Over there across the foam,
And we'll tell the story of your deeds
    Should we e'er reach Home, Sweet Home.

Sleep on! Dear fallen comrades!
    You'll ne'er be forgotten by
The boys who fought beside you
    And the boys who saw you die.

THE 3RD BATTALION'S RUM

H.W. CAVILL

There is one humorous incident connected with the famous Lone Pine charge that deserves to be recorded; that is the story of the 3rd Battalion's rum.

The officers of the 3rd Battalion were addressed by their Colonel the evening before the fight, and one of the matters that came up to be decided was that of rum. Two issues of rum were due on the day of the fight, and the question was when should they be given.

The Colonel was an old Australian soldier of the Instructional Staff—one of the finest fighters at Gallipoli. He was wounded three times in the next twenty-four hours and was carried dying from the trenches he had won.

At this conference, the night before the fight, he laid down his view: 'I believe the issue will be a good tonic to the men in their present condition,' he said, 'but I do not like the idea of giving it to men just before they go into action. We will have one issue in the morning, and the other after the fight is over.'

It was next day, about two hours after the charge, when a man with a demijohn on his shoulder came along, up Shrapnel Valley and into the firing line trenches. The Brigadier himself was at the mouth of that sap receiving messages. He was trying to clear the sap to let some of the most urgent traffic through. All traffic to the front had to pass through thirty yards of narrow, pitch-dark tunnel, and then out over the heath, facing the gauntlet up to the parapet of the Turkish trench.

Endless lines of men with ammunition, men with bombs, men with water, men with picks, shovels, sandbags, signallers, messengers, engineers, stretcher-bearers, were filing at funeral pace into it, and the whole tunnel was constantly blocked, while they carried one or two poor badly wounded fellows back.

I remember one pitiful procession that emerged from it, after at least ten minutes' struggle through the dark interior—first a seriously wounded man in a folding cane stretcher, next an army medical man, and after him, crawling on hands and knees out of the tunnel and down the trench towards the rear, another wounded man.

Only those men whose presence was urgent were allowed to go through afterwards.

'What are you carrying?'

'Bombs, sir.'

'Well, put them down here a moment, and stand by until that tunnel is clearer.'

'And what are you carrying, my man?'

'The 3rd Battalion's rum, sir.'

'What?'

'The 3rd Battalion's rum, sir. Colonel put me in charge of it, and told me to see the . . .'

'Well, put it down here, and stand by.'

'The Colonel told me to take it through, sir.'

'Well, put it down here for the present.'

'The Colonel told me . . .'

'Look here! Never mind what you were told; put it down there at once!'

The rum carrier put his heavy load down on the first step, and retired, obviously unsatisfied, for the moment. The Colonel had told him the men would want their rum, and it was his duty to see it through. For a couple of minutes he watched the Brigade staff dealing with infinitely more important messages.

Then, the first time the Brigadier looked up, he stepped forward again.

'How 'bout the 3rd Battalion's rum, sir?'

'Oh, well, get along with you,' answered the Brigadier, amusedly.

And so he shouldered it and trudged out contently towards the heath and towards the bullets, and, I suppose, the 3rd Battalion got its rum.

THOUGHTS OF HOME

ROWLEY CLARK

’Tis springtime now in the Goulburn Valley
And the wheat grows high in the distant Mallee,
And at Widgewa ’tis the lambing tally
And we’re not there.

On the Clarence banks they’re cutting the cane
On the Bowen Downs, time for milking again,
And the weights are out for the Spring campaign
And we’re not there.

On the Diamantina the cattle are lowing,
At Narrabeen now the waratah’s growing
Out on the Lachlan the billabong’s flowing
And we’re not there.

THE SECOND NURSE'S STORY

Based on various accounts, letters and diaries

The 3rd Australian General Hospital, AIF, was set up in response to a request from the British War Office.

In May 1915, the new unit sailed from Circular Quay, Sydney, with a number of Australian Army nurses. On 8 August, after travelling via Plymouth and Alexandria, forty of us were landed at the new site on Lemnos.

There was, as yet, no hospital and no accommodation—just a site pegged out on the ground and a few tents. The previous day the August offensive had begun with massive battles at Lone Pine, Rhododendron Ridge and the Nek.

Before breakfast on 9 August, more than 200 wounded arrived from Gallipoli. Four days later, there were more than 800 patients.

On 10 August a convoy of wounded arrived at night and the next day another 400 seriously wounded stretcher cases were left on the beach, most of them horribly shattered and many dying.

We had no equipment and no water to give them a drink. We could only feed them and dress their wounds; many died. The store ship didn't arrive until 20 August. There was no medical equipment whatever and no water to drink or wash. The wounded were just laid on the ground on blankets or on the floors of tents.

Even after the stores arrived conditions were awful. The travelling kitchens would burn on windy days.

The weather was terrible, bitterly cold, with wind and rain. We nearly froze, even in our balaclavas, mufflers, mittens, cardigans, raincoats and Wellingtons. We had no fruit or vegetables, and butter and eggs only once a month.

The men got dysentery from the local bread and there were scorpions and centipedes everywhere and thistles and burrs, most girls cut their hair short to save trouble. We didn't even have a bath tent.

Night after night, in the high wind, the tents would shake and flap. We lay awake waiting for them to collapse. Hardly a night passed that a tent didn't collapse.

As for the poor wounded soldiers who arrived in hundreds, the scenes were too awful to describe. It would be better for these men to be killed outright.

A LITTLE SPRIG OF WATTLE

A.H. SCOTT

My mother's letter came to-day,
And now my thoughts are far away,
For in between its pages lay
A little sprig of wattle.

'The old home now looks at its best,'
The message ran; 'the country's dressed
In spring's gay cloak, and I have pressed
A little sprig of wattle.'

I almost see that glimpse of spring:
The very air here seems to ring
With joyful notes of birds that sing
Among the sprigs of wattle.

The old home snug amidst the pines,
The trickling creek that twists and twines
Round tall gum roots and undermines,
Is all ablaze with wattle.

THE MIGHTY NEW ZEALANDERS

E.C. BULEY

The men of New Zealand had to defend the extreme left of the Australasian lines along Walker's Ridge, facing almost due north. During the month of July, too, the New Zealanders took over the defence of Quinn's Post, and by very skilful sapping operations made that once dangerous post one of the safest places in the whole camp.

Farther north than Walker's Ridge itself, the New Zealanders also held two isolated posts known as Outpost No. 1 and Outpost No. 2. Communication with the main lines from these outposts was maintained through deep saps, which had been dug by the New Zealanders themselves.

Outpost No. 2 was held by the 500 Maori and was sometimes known as Maori Outpost. This place was used as a base for stores; and here in the first days of August an immense amount of munitions and food was accumulated. At this outpost, during the night of 5 August, the men of New Zealand and the 4th Brigade of Australian infantry were massed for the attack, which began on 6 August.

Between this point and the great hill of Sari Bair (Hill 971) were a number of high points, among which were two flat-topped hills known as Greater and Lesser Tabletop and also Bauchop's Hill. The sides of these hills were almost perpendicular, and a network of trenches made them impregnable if held by any considerable force of men. In the early days of August it became known that very few men occupied these defensive trenches, and one of the objects of the attack of 6 August was to take these positions by surprise.

After dark on 6 August, the New Zealanders and the 4th Brigade of Australians marched out from Maori Outpost, stepping silently through the scrub in a northerly direction. From the beach a series of gullies, running at right angles to the shore, give an entry to the hill slopes that lead up to the main ridges of Sari Bair and Chunuk Bair, the highest points of the mountain mass separated by a deep ravine.

Up these gullies the New Zealanders made their way, clearing the enemy out of the trenches dug to bar the approaches to Sari Bair. Charging up one gully, the men of Wellington surprised and captured the Tabletop hills. Up a parallel gully the Auckland Mounted Rifles went and took possession of Rhododendron Ridge.

The Maoris charged up yet a third gully, to take Bauchop's Hill and the trenches beyond it. The fierceness of that charge, when they swept every Turk out of their path, has become legendary among the men of Anzac. The impetuosity of the charge carried them right through their own gully and into that which the men of Auckland had taken.

They came over a spur of the hills, yelling with excitement, and seeing in the dim light that a trench before them was occupied by armed men, rushed upon it, shouting their war cry. The men before them were the men of Auckland, who at once recognised the war cries of the Maoris. Fortunately the average New Zealander has a fair smattering of the Maori tongue, and the Auckland men shouted at them what phrases of Maori they could summon up in such an emergency, and the charge was stopped right on the parapet of the trench.

By such wild fighting the men of New Zealand steadily won their way upwards, through the tangle of gullies and steep hillsides toward the crest of the big hill. By day they hung on doggedly to the positions they had won, resisting attacks by bayonet and bomb. By night they moved stealthily on, through dense scrub and broken country, converging by parallel paths toward the desired crest of the hill.

No words can paint the gallantry of the fighting on those four days and 9 August saw a gallant little band of New Zealanders planting their artillery flags on the trench that spans the summit of Chunuk Bair. From that vantage point the bold pioneers could see all they had striven for through many weary weeks of constant fighting.

Away to the south-east were the forts of the Narrows. At their very feet ran the road from Gallipoli town to the main Turkish position at Achi Baba. They could see the trains of mules and the transport vehicles passing along this road. The goal of all their efforts was there, The Dardanelles, in their full sight. To their right and left, on higher crests, the Turks were massed in force, determined to drive them from Chunuk Bair.

Desperately the New Zealanders hung on to what they had gained, until support should come. Their attempt to hold that hilltop is one of the most glorious deeds in all the annals of war. Eventually the best of the Turkish commanders, Mustafa Kemal, led a huge force against them.

Finally, after sixteen New Zealanders kept a long section of trench against a whole host of enemies for three hours, the position was abandoned and the New Zealanders had to retire. Many would rather have died where they were . . . and a good many of them did so.

The losses of those four days can best be judged by reference to the casualty lists. The Auckland Mounted Rifles, 800 strong on the day of 6 August, had thirty-seven uninjured men at roll call on 11 August.

Over 400 New Zealand wounded spent those four days in a place they christened the Valley of Torment. It was a deep depression in the hillside on the rugged side of Sari Bair. On one side of it rose a perpendicular cliff that would have defied a mountain goat to climb it. On the other rose the steep declivity of Rhododendron Ridge.

The only way in and out was from above, where the New Zealanders were fighting like possessed beings for the foothold they had won on the crest of Sari Bair. Below, the valley opened out upon a flat plateau, so swept by the guns of both sides that no living thing could exist for one moment upon its flat, open surface.

To this valley the stretcher-bearers carried the men who had fallen in the fight, a sad little group of wounded men whose numbers increased hourly. Those less severely injured crawled there and unwounded soldiers carried their stricken mates there for shelter from the hail of bullets.

A devoted band of Red Cross men lent them what aid they could, stayed their wounds with bandages, tied tourniquets round limbs to check the flow of arterial blood, and made tortured men as easy as circumstances would permit. There was no doctor nearer then the dressing station on the beach.

The approach to this valley was so dangerous to attempt by daylight and there was no water there, until one man dug into a moist spot far down the valley, and chanced on a spring that yielded a trickle of brackish water.

By midday on 8 August, 300 men, suffering from all the terrible manglings that exploding bombs and high explosive shells can inflict, were in this place of refuge, and more were continually arriving. Some sought to cheer the rest by predicting a great victory as the result of the attack. Here and there a man could be heard reciting verses to those who would listen.

No one moaned, and no one uttered a complaint. When a man died of his wounds they expressed their thanks that he had been spared further pain. As the little spring filled, each man would have his lips moistened with the brackish water.

When night at last came, the weary stretcher-bearers tried to move some of them over the ridge to a safer valley on the other side. But these men had been working for days and nights without rest and the task was beyond their strength, for the steepness and roughness of that hillside is beyond description.

The next day came with a hot sun, and clouds of flies. Also there came many more wounded to the Valley of Torment, until the number exceeded 400.

That day many died and among those who lived, the torture from tourniquets that had been left too long on wounded limbs became unendurable. Many of them will never recover the free use of their limbs.

At last that day ended, too, and evening brought a cool breeze. Then they heard, from the safe gully that lay beyond the ridge, the stealthy approach of many men in the dark. One of them, out of thankfulness, began to sing the hymn—

> At even, 'ere the sun was set,
> The sick, O Lord, around Thee lay.

Nearly all of them took up the singing and, while they were still singing, over the ridge came a large number of soldiers who put them all on stretchers. The newcomers, some thousands in number, ranged themselves in two rows that stretched up the crest of the ridge and down the other side into the safe gully.

Each stretcher was passed from hand to hand, to the safety on the other side where a long procession was formed, bearing the wounded down to the sea. Two miles it stretched from start to finish and so the wounded men of New Zealand were carried out of the Valley of Torment.

I have met many of the men who suffered there; and I know that in their eyes the real tragedy is not the torture they experienced. It is that their comrades eventually had to withdraw from the hilltops that had been won by so much loss of life.

One wounded corporal told me his story:

We lay under cover in the dark waiting for the word to go. Every man had his bayonet fixed and his magazine empty. The work before us had to be done with cold steel. The Turks had three lines of trenches on the hill slope opposite.

Suddenly I became aware of a stir among the Maoris on my left; I was right up against them. Next to me was a full-blooded Maori chief, a young fellow of sixteen stone, as big and powerful as a bullock, a lineal descendant of fighting Rewi, the Maori chief from whom all the legends descend.

This fellow has two good university degrees and is a lay preacher. I once saw him in a frock coat and silk hat, talking on the virtues of cleanliness and the nobility of hard work.

But now he had dressed for the occasion in a pair of running shoes and shorts, which covered about eight inches of the middle of him. I could see his brown skin glistening with perspiration in the dim light as we waited for the whistle to blow and send us over the top. His head was moving from side to side and his lips were twitching. From time to time he beat the earth softly with his clenched fist.

Then I got the rhythm of it and realised what was happening. I suppose those 500 Maoris picked me up into their silent war song.

I know the words of the Haka well, and though they could not dance it they were beating out the measure of it with their fists on the ground. After each soft thump I could feel that their bodies strained forward like dogs on a leash. They caught me up in their madness and I longed to be at it. I thumped the ground with them, and prayed to be up and dancing, or out and fighting.

Their eyes were rolling and their breath was coming in long, rhythmical sobs. The groaning sound of it was quite audible; in another minute they would have been up on their feet, dancing their wild war dance. But then came the signal; and Hell was let loose.

'Ake, Ake,' they shouted, 'we fight for ever and for ever.'

Up to the first trench they swept. I could hear some of them yelling, 'Kiki ta Turk'. Those were the fellows who had kept on their heaviest boots, and meant to use their feet. God help the Turk who got a kick from a war-mad Maori.

Our blood was up; I know mine was. We were not far behind them to the first trench, and you never saw such a sight in your life.

The Turks had been bashed to death; there is no other word for it. We got up to them at the second trench, where there was a deadly hand-to-hand going on. Some of them had broken their rifles and were fighting with their hands. I saw one Maori smash a Turk with half-a-hundredweight of rock he had torn up.

I don't remember much more, because I was in the thick of it myself by then, that's why I am here in the hospital.

I don't know anything more at first-hand but I hear a good many of them came back, though I shouldn't have thought it possible. The Turks who escaped will not wait next time when they hear the Maoris coming . . . and you can hear them coming all right.

THE ANZAC V.C.s

OLIVER HOGUE

Our first Australian V.C. was Jacka of the 4th Brigade. He was young and didn't have the splendid tall physique of most of the Australians, but he was greased lightning with the bayonet. It all happened on Courtney's Post. The Turks had been sapping in towards the front trench, and after a shower of bombs they swarmed in and captured the trench. Lance Corporal Jacka, posted behind the traverse in the fire trench, blocked their advance. An officer and a few men hurried up and volunteers were immediately ready to eject the intruders.

Then, while the officer and three men engaged in a bombing exchange with the enemy, Albert Jacka jumped from the front trench into the communication trench behind, ran round and took the Turks in the rear. He shot five of them and bayoneted two. The officer's party then charged and shot the four remaining Turks who tried to escape. They found Jacka leaning up against the side of the trench with flushed face, a bloody bayonet in the end of his rifle and an unlighted cigarette in his mouth.

The boys who took Lone Pine in that fine charge, amid a shower of lead and shrapnel such as the war had not previously seen, got no V.C. for their valour. But the lads who held the hard-won post against all the subsequent counter-attacks did manage to secure a few. One of these was Captain Shout. But he never lived to wear the cross. For three long days and longer nights he participated in the furious hand-to-hand fighting in Lone Pine.

Captain Shout with his bombing gang was ubiquitous. Laughing and cheering them on he time and again drove the Turks back, and then when he reached a point where the final sandbag barrier was to be erected, he tried to light three bombs at once and throw them amongst the crowding Turks. To throw a single bomb is a risky job. To throw three bombs simultaneously was a desperate expedient. One exploded prematurely, shattered both his hands, laid open his cheek and destroyed an eye, besides minor injuries. Conscious and still cheerful he was carried away. But he died shortly afterwards.

The heroic 7th Battalion—victorious Victorians—participated in the great charge of the 2nd Australian Infantry Brigade down at Helles, the charge that made the French and English marvel at the dash of the young colonials. Four men of the 7th Battalion—Captain Fred Tubb, Lieutenant Symons, Corporal Dunstan and Corporal Burton—won the V.C. at Lone Pine.

On the night of 8 August, while the British troops in the Suvla area were struggling to wrest the hills from the Turks, the Turks round Lone Pine were vainly endeavouring to recapture this stronghold from the Australians. On the right of the 7th Battalion, things were particularly sultry, and early on the morning of the ninth some determined attacks resulted in six of our officers and several men being killed and wounded. A bit of the front sap was lost, but Lieutenant Symons headed a charge, retook the sap, shot two of the Turks with his revolver and finally erected a barricade which defied all the attacks of the enemy who set fire to the overhead cover in the hope of driving back the 7th. But the fire was extinguished and the position held for good.

It was give and take, attack and counter-attack all through 9 August that showed the qualities of pluck and determination, which won the V.C. for Captain F.H. Tubb, Corporal Dunstan and Corporal Burton. Three times the enemy attacked with bombs, blew up our barricades, and swarmed into the trench, but each time Tubb and his companions returned to the assault, repulsed the invaders, rebuilt the barricades, and in spite of a shower of bombs held the post. Captain Tubb was wounded in the head and arm, but stuck to his job throughout.

Lance Corporal Keyzor was one of a band of heroes who did wonders in the hell-zone at the south-eastern corner of Lone Pine. It was a murder hole and after much slaughter we found that we could not hold the outer trench, while the enemy found that he also was unable to hold it. Finally it was abandoned as No Man's Land.

As a bomb-thrower, Keyzor was pre-eminent. He was one of those who repeatedly caught the enemy's bombs and hurled them back before they could explode. It was here that Colonel Scobie was killed shortly afterwards, and here it was that for days and nights Keyzor moved amongst the showers of bombs with dead and dying all around, and threw bombs till every muscle ached and he could not lift his arm.

John Hamilton was very young, just nineteen. But lots of these young Australians had old heads on their young shoulders. It was at Lone Pine, where the 3rd Battalion was defending a section of the line against the repeated attacks of the Turks, that young Hamilton won the coveted honour. He climbed on to the top of the parapet and with a few sandbags as a precarious shield against bombs and bullets he stayed there for five solid hours sniping merrily, potting off any stray Turks that showed up, and giving warning to the officer below each time the enemy started out to attack. There was plenty of shrapnel flying and the zip of bullets into the sandbags grew monotonous. But young Hamilton hung on.

It was away on the left of our line at Hill 60 that Lieutenant Throssell of the 10th Light Horse performed his great act of valour. There was one section of the enemy's line that obstinately defied the Australasian attack. At last the 3rd Light Horse Brigade received orders that the redoubt had to be taken. The Brigadier sent the 10th Light Horse Regiment out to do the job.

***

Just after midnight—28–29 August—the Westralians suddenly leaped on to the parapet and charged ahead. They were met with a hail of machine-gun and rifle fire and a shower of bombs, but nothing could stop those horseless horsemen. A brief melee on and in the Turkish trenches and the position was won. But holding it was a far more difficult matter. Lieutenant Throssell, in charge of the digging party, worked overtime putting the new line in a state of defence.

Soon the Turks massed for the inevitable counter-attack, and Throssell, with Captain Fry and a troop of the Light Horse, repulsed the first charge. But just as dawn was breaking the Turks came again with a shower of bombs as a prelude. The grenades were smothered as they fell or were thrown back again, but Captain Fry paid the final penalty. One bomb rolled over the parapet into the trench, and spluttered. The men yelled, 'Let it rip.' But the only safe thing to do was to smother the bomb or heave it out. The gallant Captain chose the latter alternative, but the bomb exploded and killed him.

The holding of this threatened elbow of the line devolved upon Throssell, who rose manfully to the occasion. With his rifle he shot half a dozen Turks and with his cheery example he heartened his command, and the enemy attacked in vain. Twice indeed they swarmed in and the Light Horsemen had to give ground. But only a few yards and a fresh barricade was immediately erected. Early in the afternoon Throssell was wounded in the shoulder. But he kept on. At four o'clock he got another bullet in the neck, but still he kept on. Just after nightfall relief came and his superior officer sent him back to the field hospital.

There were other Australians who gained the V.C., Captain William Cosgrove of the Royal Munster Fusiliers, who did such a fine performance down at Helles, and others. But other historians will tell of their deeds. Corporal Bassett of the New Zealand Signallers won his V.C. for a daring exploit—laying a telephone wire right on to Chunuk Bair in broad daylight under a heavy fire.

Scores of the boys did big things that in lesser wars would have won distinction. Here they just were numbered with the unknown heroes. Every man on Lone Pine deserved special honour.

If they had been Germans they would have been covered with Iron Crosses. As it is they are just satisfied that they were able to do their job. Anyhow, Australia won't forget Lone Pine.

'WE'RE ALL AUSTRALIANS NOW'

A.B. 'BANJO' PATERSON

Published as an open letter to the troops, 1915

Australia takes her pen in hand,
To write a line to you,
To let you fellows understand,
How proud we are of you.

From shearing shed and cattle run,
From Broome to Hobson's Bay,
Each native-born Australian son,
Stands straighter up today.

The man who used to 'hump his drum',
On far-out Queensland runs,
Is fighting side by side with some
Tasmanian farmer's sons.

The fisher-boys dropped sail and oar
To grimly stand the test,
Along that storm-swept Turkish shore,
With miners from the west.

The old state jealousies of yore
Are dead as Pharaoh's sow,
We're not State children any more
We're all Australians now!

Our six-starred flag that used to fly,
Half-shyly to the breeze,
Unknown where older nations ply
Their trade on foreign seas,

Flies out to meet the morning blue
With Vict'ry at the prow;
For that's the flag the *Sydney* flew,
The wide seas know it now!

The mettle that a race can show,
Is proved with shot and steel,
And now we know what nations know
And feel what nations feel.

The honoured graves beneath the crest
Of Gaba Tepe hill,
May hold our bravest and our best,
But we have brave men still.

With all our petty quarrels done,
Dissensions overthrown,
We have, through what you boys have done,
A history of our own.

Our old world diff'rences are dead,
Like weeds beneath the plough,
For English, Scotch, and Irish-bred,
They're all Australians now!

So now we'll toast the Third Brigade,
That led Australia's van,
For never shall their glory fade
In minds Australian.

Fight on, fight on, unflinchingly,
Till right and justice reign.
Fight on, fight on, till Victory
Shall send you home again.

And with Australia's flag shall fly
A spray of wattle bough,
To symbolise our unity,
We're all Australians now.

THE FINAL PHASE

After the August offensive another stalemate eventuated; not one inch of territory was won or conceded by the Anzac forces from the end of August until they were evacuated in December.

By the end of August more than 80 per cent of the Allied troops were suffering from dysentery. Then winter brought snow and many soldiers died from exposure or suffered frostbite.

The Allied troops at Anzac Cove and Suvla Bay were withdrawn in December 1915. Unlike the landings and the eight-month siege campaign, the evacuation was a masterpiece of military strategy and coordination.

Troops were evacuated steadily from 11 December, and the final 20,000 left furtively and completely undetected on 18 and 19 December.

A rear-guard of 1500 men occupied the trenches and fired rifles, made noises and set timers on guns and booby traps to make it appear that the trenches were occupied as normal. On a given signal the rear-guard ran to the deserted beach and were taken off under cover of darkness.

Only two lives were lost during the whole process of evacuation.

Anzac and Suvla were evacuated by 20 December 1915. The British forces at Cape Helles, however, remained in place until 7 January and were evacuated on 8 and 9 January 1916.

ANZAC ALPHABET

'IFSH'

A is for Anzac, renowned evermore,
B is for Beachy who bursts on the shore.
C is for Colic which follows directly,
D is for Dose taken paregorectly.
E is for Exercise climbing the hills,
F for Fatigues which come faster than bills.
G is the German who makes the Turk fight,
H is for Hell which we hope is his plight.
I is for Indian, excellent fellow,
J is for Jaundice which makes us turn yellow.
K is for Kobber, Australian for friend,
L the Last Post which comes right at the end.
M is for Mule who's as game as a sparrow,
N is the Nuisance of saps much too narrow.
O is for Oaths, some of which are ripsnorters,
P is the Pain they produce at headquarters.
Q is the Quiver that runs down your back,
R the big Rooster which shells from Chanak
S the Soft Jobs you get back at base,
T is for Turk who's a pretty tough case.
U is for Underground where we all rest,
V is for Vickers, the man-killing pest.
W the Whisky we sigh for in vain,
X for Xcitement, 'The mail's in again!'
Y is for 'Yes' if we're asked to go home,
Z is for Zero, we're chilled to the bone!

WINTER ARRIVES

H.W. DINNING

It is now late October and autumn and changes in temperature are as incalculable as they are in Melbourne in certain seasons. Fierce, biting, raw days alternate with the comfortableness of mild late summer. Today it may be more than your life is worth to bathe (shrapnel disregarded) and tomorrow in the gentle air you may swim and splash for an hour and still desire more as you prolong the joy by washing your garments in the ocean.

We have suffered the tail end of one or two autumn storms and have had two downright fierce gales blow up where the wind came in the night with a suddenness that found most unprepared. In half an hour many of us were homeless, crouching about with our bundled bedclothes and trespassing on the confined space of the stouter dug-outs of our friends.

Men lay on their backs and held down their roofs by the weight of their bodies until overpowered and the sea roared over the shingle beach with a violence that made even swearing and blasphemy inaudible.

For weeks men had been preparing dug-outs against the approach of winter, but they were unprepared for weather of such violence. The morning showed a sorry sight on the beach, barges torn adrift from their moorings and hurled ashore. Some were empty, some were filled with supplies; but all were battered, some disabled and some utterly broken. One was filled with rum and never before, on active service, had such a chance of unlimited spirits been offered. Many jars were spirited away before the time of unloading came.

Far more serious was the state of the landing piers. There had been three. One stood intact; the landward half of the second was clean gone and of the third there was no trace except a few splintered spars on the shore.

The mending began forthwith but so did the bursting of shrapnel over the workmen, for this stroke of vengeance from Allah upon the unfaithful was not to go unsupplemented.

By nightfall, however, the abridged pier was successfully reunited with the shore, in spite of the shrapnel and a sea that made it impossible for barges to come alongside.

For two days the after-wind of the gale kept bread and meat and mail tossing on the waters off Anzac and we were fed on bully beef and biscuit as we wistfully eyed the mail trawler pitching out there with her precious burden. For the arrival of mail eclipses all other considerations, even life and death, the fighting or even the landing of rations!

Mail has been arriving weekly for six months. Sometimes it comes twice a week, for the Army Corps Post Office never rests and instalments may be spread over three or four landings.

Most mails are landed between sunset and dawn, mostly after midnight. Post Office officials must be there to check and supervise and they get little sleep on 'mail nights'.

Incoming mails do not constitute all their work; outgoing mail from the firing line is heavy and they have other tasks to perform also.

There are the pathetic 'returns' to be dealt with, the letters to men who will never read them, written before the heavy news had reached home. A huge bulk of correspondence is marked 'Killed' and re-addressed to the place of origin of the fallen soldiers. Their comrades keep their newspapers and the parcels of comforts bring melancholy cheer to their fighting comrades-in-arms. What else is to be done with them?

Letters put a man at home for a couple of hours, and so does his local newspaper. Perusing the local paper takes him back to the old habit of picking at the news over his eggs and coffee or on the suburban business train. Intimate associations hang about the reading of the local newspaper, associations almost as powerful as are brought by letters. If relatives at home understood this they would despatch newspapers with stricter regularity.

And what can be said about parcels from home? No son away at boarding school ever pursued his voyage of discovery through tarts, cakes, sweets, pies and fruit with the intensity of gloating expectation that a man on Gallipoli displays as he discloses the contents of his 'parcel'.

'Strewth, Bill, look, a new pipe! And some of me favourite terbaccer. Blimey, cigars too! Have one before the crowd smells 'em. Hello, more socks! Oh well, winter's comin'. 'Ere, 'ow are you orf for socks, cobber? Take these, bonzer hand-knitted, sling them army issue things into the sea . . . Gawd! 'ere's a shaving stick, that's handy . . . I clean run out of carbolic soap!'

Mail deserves all the organised care the War Office can bestow; mail makes for efficiency.

There may be no morning delivery of the daily newspaper on Anzac, but we get the news. At the foot of Headquarters Gully is the notice board and wireless messages are posted daily. At any hour men are elbowing their way into the perusing circle.

There is news of operations along our own front and copious messages from the Russian and Western fronts. The Melbourne Cup finish was cabled through immediately. There were few men who did not handle their purses around the board that evening, for no war news, for months, had been so momentous as this.

The associations called to mind by the news from Flemington were strong and homely, as well as national. Men were recalled for a while from the land of blood and death to the office, the bank, the warehouse, the country pub or the shearing shed where Cup bets were often placed and sweeps made. The sporting spirit is stronger than any other Australian national trait. The Defence Department knew what they were doing when they made provision for a cabled despatch of the running of the Cup to Gallipoli.

ON POST

'TAMBOUR 8'

Peepin' through a loophole during weary hours of night
Listenin' till yer eardrums nearly crack.
Waitin' for the Corporal to bring the new relief,
Bendin' till the pains run down your back;
Starin' till your eyeballs are just about to roll,
What a lovely life for men to lead;
Who would be on sentry post along the Anzac line,
With bully beef and biscuits for yer feed?
Standin' up with leaden feet and toes that can't be felt;
Boots wet through and stickin' to the bank—
Nose tip like the apex of a blanky icicle,
Hair all wet and clingin' thick and dank:
Teeth that chatter freely in the bitter bitin' cold,
Jove! I used ter think that home was bad,
Now I'm doing sentry post along the Anzac line
Strewth! A bloomin' bloke like me is mad.
When the flamin' snow came down the other blanky night
I was draped in white from head to feet;
I musta been a picture to the officer of the watch,
When he came along to do his beat.
When I think of all me pals and cobbers stayin' home
And all the things us blokes have given up;
How I'm freezing doing sentry post along the Anzac line
When I mighta been in Melbourne for The Cup.
But, what's the good of grumblin' at blokes that stayed at home?
When I think of mates like Jim and Ted,

Down in Shrapnel Gully with a little wooden cross,
It sorta makes me cooler in the head.
I'm still doing sentry post along the Anzac line,
But, maybe, when I've seen me last big 'show',
I'll be down there in the gully somewhere near me two old pals,
And that's the last 'rest post' to which I'll go.

FROSTBITE

OLIVER HOGUE

Days dragged drearily on. Pessimism peeped into the trenches. Later, in the solitude of the dug-out, pessimism stayed an unwelcome guest, and would not be banished. All the glorious optimism of April, the confidence of May, June and July had gone, and the dogged determination of August, September and October was fast petering out. The Turks had fringed the dominating hills with barbed wire and bayonets, and in very surety Australia was 'up against it'.

Not that anyone dared talk pessimism. The croakers would have been squelched instantly. But deep down there was a feeling that unless heavy reinforcements arrived we could never break through to Constantinople. But at Helles, Anzac and Suvla the British hung on, desperately, heroically.

September's cold snap was forgotten in the unexpected warmth of October—just like an afterglow of summer. Then came the wintry winds of November—and the blizzard . . . Of course we have snow in Australia. Kosciusko is all the year round covered with a soft white mantle. Down on Monaro it can be bleak and wintry. And the old Blue Mountains now and then enjoy a spell of sleet and snow . . . But taking us by and large we are a warm-blooded race, we Australians. That is why we viewed the approach of winter with some concern.

We knew the Turks could never, never, never break through our lines, and drive us—as Liman von Sanders had boasted—into the sea. But we were beginning to fear that we were a long, long way from Constantinople.

The blizzard swooped down on Anzac. Just like a shroud the white visitation settled on Gallipoli. It was cold as a Monaro gale. Soldiers crowded round the fires, and at night in the trenches it was terribly hard to keep awake.

The cold was something to remember. We could keep our hands a bit warm by giving 'five rounds rapid' and hugging the rifle barrel. Talk about cold feet; we had heard of 'cold feet' when we were in Egypt, but this was the real thing.

How we invoked rich blessings on the heads of the Australian girls who had knitted us those warm socks! How we cursed the thieves along the lines of communication who pillaged and pilfered, while the men in the firing line went begging! But through it all the indomitable cheerfulness of the Australian soldier would not be crushed. They laughed and joked when their teeth chattered, so that clear articulation was impossible.

To preserve some circulation they stamped their feet till exhaustion bade them cease. But the blizzard was inexorable. The cold permeated everywhere. We got just a glimpse of what the British Army suffered in the Crimea.

Frostbite was something to fear and dread. It was agonising. Hundreds of men were carried down to the field hospitals and sent across to Lemnos. There were scores of amputations daily . . . We had cursed the heat of July and the plague of flies, but now we prayed for summer again.

SONG OF A SOCK

ANONYMOUS

It was forbidden for women knitting articles for Red Cross parcels to include any identification or messages. This poem is based on one that was found in a pair of socks.

***

Knitted in the tram-car,
Knitted in the street,
Knitted by the fireside,
Knitted in the heat;
Knitted in Australia
Where the gum tree grows,
Sent to you at Anzac,
Just to warm your toes.

Knitted here and knitted there
With this soft refrain,
'May the one who wears them
Come back to us again'.

Knitted by the seaside,
Knitted in the train,
Knitted in the sunshine,
Knitted in the rain.

Knitted in Springtime
Where the wattle grows,
Sent to some brave soldier,
Out at Anzac Cove.

Knitted here and knitted there
With this soft refrain,
'May the one who wears them
Come back to us again'.

THE GREATEST PRIVILEGE

JIM HAYNES

Much of the myth-building about Gallipoli comes from an 8000-word letter written by twenty-nine-year-old journalist Keith Murdoch in September 1915.

Murdoch was born in Melbourne on 12 August 1885 and became a journalist with the *Age*. In 1911 he was promoted and became Commonwealth parliamentary reporter and was a founding member of the Australian Journalists Association, established in 1910.

When the First World War began Murdoch narrowly lost the ballot for the coveted position of official correspondent to the AIF (which went to Charles Bean) and he went to London to become Managing Editor of the United Cable Service, which serviced all Australian newspapers.

Murdoch was at the Dardanelles for less than a week, just after the August fighting, and he then spent time with the war correspondents an Imbros, where the British journalist Ellis Ashmead Bartlett asked him to take a letter to the British prime minister without passing the censor.

Murdoch was arrested when the letter, scathingly critical of the Gallipoli campaign, was intercepted and confiscated at Marseilles, but he wrote an 8000-word letter of his own and sent it to Andrew Fisher, the Australian prime minister. The letter is credited with contributing to the decision to evacuate and the recall of General Sir Ian Hamilton, the campaign's commander.

Murdoch called the campaign 'undoubtedly one of the most terrible chapters in our history'. He claimed that officers and men had 'nothing but contempt' for Hamilton and the general staff and stated:

> Undoubtedly the essential and first step to restore the morale of the shaken forces is to recall [Hamilton] and his Chief of Staff [Lieutenant General Sir W.P. Braithwaite], a man more cordially detested in our forces than Enver Pasha [the Turkish war minister] . . . It is not for me to judge Hamilton, but it is plain that when an Army has completely lost faith in its General, and he has on numerous occasions proved his weaknesses, only one thing can be done.

Commenting on the failure of the forces at Suvla to advance, he declared: 'The spirit at Suvla is simply deplorable. You would refuse to believe that these are really British soldiers.'

The letter went on to claim that the forces at Suvla were 'simply a lot of child-like youths' who showed 'an atrophy of mind and body that is appalling'.

On the other hand, Murdoch was convinced that the Turk was 'a brave and generous foe'.

Chancellor of the Exchequer, Lloyd George, who opposed the Gallipoli campaign, read the letter and immediately urged that Murdoch send a copy to the British prime minister, Asquith.

Without checking the allegations or asking Hamilton for his comments, Asquith had the letter printed as a state paper and circulated to the members of the Dardanelles Committee, which was in charge of the campaign. Hamilton was recalled and the new commander, General Charles Monro, suggested evacuation, which began on 12 December 1915.

A Royal Commission, at which Murdoch and Ashmead-Bartlett both gave evidence, began sitting in August 1916 and found that the campaign had been a mistake.

In 1921 Murdoch became chief editor of the Melbourne evening *Herald* and, in 1929, he acquired the *Adelaide Advertiser* and established the Murdoch media dynasty.

Murdoch's praise of the Australian troops became the catalyst for much of the almost-sacred high regard Australians quickly developed for our men at Gallipoli. He talked of 'the grandeur of our Australian army and the wonderful affection of these fine young soldiers for each other and their homeland' and told Prime Minister Fisher that, if he could tell him how they behaved, his 'Australianism would become a more powerful sentiment than before'.

'Oh, if you could picture Anzac as I have seen it,' he told Andrew Fisher, 'you would find that to be an Australian is the greatest privilege the world has to offer.'

THE AUSTRALIAN, 'THE BRAVEST THING GOD EVER MADE!'

WILL OGILVIE

A British Officer's Opinion of the Australians at Gallipoli

The skies that arched his land were blue,
His bush-born winds were warm and sweet,
And yet from earliest hours he knew
The tides of victory and defeat:
From fierce floods thundering at his birth,
From red droughts ravening while he played,
He learned to fear no foes on earth—
The bravest thing God ever made!

The bugles of the Motherland
Rang ceaselessly across the sea,
To call him and his lean brown band
To shape Imperial destiny.
He went by youth's grave purpose willed,
The goal unknown, the cost unweighed,
The promise of his blood fulfilled—
The bravest thing God ever made!

We know—it is our deathless pride!
The splendour of his first fierce blow;
How, reckless, glorious, undenied,
He stormed those steel-lined cliffs we know!

And none who saw him scale the height
Behind his reeking bayonet blade
Would rob him of his title right—
The bravest thing God ever made!

Bravest, where half a world of men
Are brave beyond all earth's rewards,
So stoutly none shall charge again
Till the last breaking of the swords;
Wounded or hale, won home from war,
Or yonder by the Lone Pine laid,
Give him his due for evermore—
The bravest thing God ever made!

EVACUATION

OLIVER HOGUE

N ow and then the English home papers blew in and we eagerly
scanned the pages of the dailies for news of the war. We were
astounded at the tone of the criticism hurled at the Government.
So much of it was Party criticism, captious criticism. So little of it
was helpful constructive criticism.

In Parliament and in the Press the critics were 'agin the
Gov'ment' rather than against the Hun. We felt wonderfully proud
of the commendable restraint of our politicians. Not one word of
captious criticism had there come from responsible Australian
papers and people.

We knew that mistakes had been made. We knew that it was a
big gamble sending the fleet to hammer their way through without
the aid of an army. But we did not slang-wang the Government.
In the dark hour when everybody was blaming everybody there
was only one message from Australia. Press and politicians struck
the same note. It was merely a reiteration of the Prime Minister's
message that the last man and the last shilling in Australia were
now and always at the disposal of the Empire.

Then came talk of evacuation. It staggered us. In the House of
Commons and in the Press columns were devoted to discussing
the Dardanelles question and evacuation was freely recommended.
The Australians rose in wrath and exclaimed, 'We're d****d if we'll
evacuate. We are going to see this game through.' It was unthinkable
that, having put our hands to the plough, we could turn back.

The Turks and their German masters were kept well informed
of the discussions at home and it made them tremendously cocky.

England had practically admitted failure. The great Dardanelles expedition—the greatest crusade in the world—was an admitted fiasco. Then the Turks reasoned together. And they agreed that even 'the fool English' would never talk so much about evacuation if it were even remotely likely. But it was worth an army corps to Abdul, and it did not make General Birdwood's task any easier.

Then Kitchener came. Many of us had seen him in Australia and South Africa. We had confidence that he would see the thing through. He landed on the beach and soon the word buzzed through the dug-outs, up the gully, and along the firing line. 'K of K' was on Anzac and the boys off duty congregated to give him a rousing welcome. He went round the Anzac defences with General Birdwood, saw everything and then started in to weigh the pros and cons of a knotty problem.

Ever since the day of landing, we had discussed in an offhand way the possibility of 'getting out'. Not that we had ever considered it remotely possible that we should ever turn back. But just as a strategical and tactical exercise, we had figured out how it might be done. And it seemed that the job of getting out was fraught with more potentialities of disaster than the job of getting in.

The landing on 25 April was responsible for some slaughter. The evacuation, we reckoned, would be carnage. At a most moderate computation twenty-five per cent of the Australian and New Zealand Army Corps would have to be sacrificed to ensure the safe withdrawal of the remainder. But of course this was only a theoretical exercise. It was really outside the sphere of practical politics.

WHEN WE RETURN

E.P. McCARTHY

What hand could write the gladness that waits us on the day?
We say farewell to Anzac and steam across her bay.
When all the fighting's over in this long cruel war
And we are rocking southward, beyond the Grecian shore.
When Imbros lies behind us and Lemnos fades from view,
When Suvla Bay's forgotten, and Achi Baba too.
When Lone Pine is a mem'ry that's fading from us fast,
And Khalid Bahr's becoming a nightmare of the past.
When we have left the trenches and dugouts on the hill,
Each heart will leap as never we thought men's heart could thrill.
Away from horrid mem'ries of death moans and of pain.
God speed the twenty-knotter that takes us home again.
And to the coast of Egypt, with sun haze on the sand,
While racing down the Suez, we'll wave a farewell hand:
We'll cast no backward glances across the Indian Sea,
Our thoughts will fly before us and light of heart we'll be.
And when the big boat's nearing her berth by Sydney quay,
And two black eyes are watching the side rails there for me,
Oh, let them drop the anchor and get the gangway down!
And let us see the land again in our old Sydney town.
We'll kiss the girls who waited through those long years so true.
Our patient loving sisters and grey haired mothers too.
We'll find familiar faces and friends on every hand
When we return . . . if we return . . . to that sweet southern land.

A SILENT GETAWAY

OLIVER HOGUE

Then like a bomb came word that in very surety we were going to evacuate. In the House of Commons members had asked in an airy way why the troops were not withdrawn from Suvla and Anzac.

To them, in their ignorance, it was merely a matter of embarking again and returning to Egypt or Salonica or France. So simple it seemed to those armchair strategists. They did not know that the beach at Anzac, our main depots, and our headquarters were within a thousand yards of the main Turkish line; that the beach had been constantly shelled by 'Beachy Bill' and other batteries for eight solid months on end.

However, the powers that be had so ordained it and that was sufficient. The Australians had talked about 'never retreating', but that was only a manifestation of the unconquerable spirit that animated them. They might talk, but they never yet disobeyed an order. It nearly broke their hearts to leave the spot where so many thousand gallant young Australians had found heroes' graves; but they knew how to obey orders. The only kick was for the honour of being the last to leave. So many wanted to be amongst the 'diehards'.

It was to be a silent 'get-away'. Absolute secrecy was essential for its success. It sounds just like a wild bit of fiction. Just imagine the possibility of withdrawing an army of 90,000 men with artillery, stores, field hospitals, mules and horses, and all the vast impedimenta of war, right from under the nose of an active enemy, and all on a clear moonlit night. One single traitor could have queered the whole pitch. But British, Indians, New Zealanders and Australians were loyal to the core.

The final attack of the Turks on the right of our line had been repulsed by the 2nd Light Horse Brigade, though the enemy in determined fashion had pushed forward with sandbags right to within a few yards of our trenches.

There were half a dozen spots in the Anzac firing line where we and the Turks could hear each other talking: Quinn's Post, Lone Pine, the Nek, Apex, Turkish Despair, Chatham's Post. It would be fine fun sticking it out here while the army made its get-away. Men clamoured for the honour of being the last to leave . . .

It is the night of 19 December; the fatal night which will see the evacuation of Anzac. Men talked cheerily, but thought hard. Had the Turks any idea of our projected departure? Two nights ago, a little after midnight, there was an unrehearsed incident. A fire broke out in a depot near North Beach. Soon the whole sky was reddened with the glare and the rugged outline of Anzac was brightly illuminated. Bully beef and biscuits blazed merrily. Oil drums burst with terrific force.

Then we wondered if the Turks would deduce anything from this. Would they guess it was a preliminary to the 'get-away'? It was hardly likely. The 'fool English' would never burn the stores till the last minute. So the accidental fire did no harm. Maybe it did good. For during the past month the Anzacs had tried by all manner of tricks and subterfuges to induce Abdul to attack. But Abdul knew how costly a business it was attacking the Australians, and after a few abortive attempts he remained on the defensive . . .

Now all was normal. Down at Helles the British had, during the afternoon, made a big demonstration. The warships had joined in the fray and the bombardment of the Turkish lines was terrific. But on this last night there was nothing untoward happening.

General Birdwood during the day had gone the rounds of the trenches and the boys yarned with him as of old. It was a good thing for us to have had a General like that—one who understood the devil-may-care Australian character. That's why the boys called him the 'idol of Anzac'.

***

Away to the northward at Suvla on the shoulder of Chocolate Hills the British divisions are getting ready to retire. On Hill 60, which saw so much sanguinary fighting, the stolid Indians are awaiting orders. This way a bit, the New Zealand and Australian Division has started its first parties towards North Beach. On the right above Anzac and opposite Gaba Tepe the Australians were streaming away, all but the rear-guard and the final 'diehards'.

Before the morning Anzac will have seen a great tragedy, or else the greatest bluff in history . . . There is the usual desultory interchange of musketry at odd places along the line, now and then punctuated with the rattle of a maxim . . . nothing abnormal. Down at Helles there is a fierce fusillade. This will help us . . .

Since dusk the first contingents had been steadily streaming down towards North Beach and Anzac Cove. Quickly and silently they embarked in the waiting flotilla of small craft and streaked out to the transports. Like guardian angels the warships hovered around seeing to the security of the army.

Up at Suvla we knew similar scenes were being enacted. Along the line the musketry played its usual accompaniment to the intermittent bombing. But the whole plan was working beautifully. The tension was gradually relaxing. There would be no twenty per cent casualties as the pessimists foretold. Already from Suvla and Anzac over 60,000 soldiers had re-embarked without a single casualty.

Now and then there was a round of shrapnel sent by Beachy Bill on to the southern depot at Brighton Beach. This clearly showed that the enemy suspected nothing. Yet it is bright moonlight . . . It is midnight, and nearly all the men have embarked save the thin khaki line of 'diehards' in the trenches.

An odd bomb or two is thrown by the Turks. Then from the Apex, after a final volley, streaked the first batch of the skeleton rear-guard. There is a breach in the brave Anzac line at last. But Abdul does not know it yet. Soon the daredevils at Quinn's Post heave a few bombs, then silently slink back, down the precipitous hillside, and along the gully to the beach.

From Courtney's and the Nek and the Pimple and Ryrie's Post and Chatham's all along the line came the 'diehards', full lick to the beach. But to their unutterable surprise there is no attack. They are not followed. The trenches that for eight long months defied the Turkish attacks are now open, not a solitary soldier left. But Abdul does not know it. There is still an intermittent fire from the Turkish trenches. They think our silence is some trick . . .

At half past three on the morning of 20 December there was a burst of red flame and a roar like distant thunder. This was repeated shortly afterwards, and our two big mines on the Neck blew up. It was our last slap at the Turk. We cannot say what harm it did, but thinking the explosions were a prelude to attack the Turkish line all round Anzac burst into spiteful protest. There was a wild fusillade at our empty trenches, and on the transports the Australians smiled grimly.

Shortly afterwards the Light Horsemen on the extreme right— Ryrie's lucky 2nd Brigade rear-guard—entered the waiting cutters on Brighton Beach. Then the stores—such as we could not take away—burst into flame. Only two men were wounded.

Before dawn word came that the whole force had been safely taken off, together with many of the mules and horses and guns, which it was thought, would have to be abandoned. At dawn the Turkish batteries opened a wild bombardment of our trenches, all along the line. Marvellous to relate, the enemy had not yet ascertained what had happened. But the silence soon told them the truth. Then they charged in irregular lines over the skyline at our empty trenches.

The warships fired a few salvoes at the enemy swarming over the hills, and they hurriedly took cover in our old trenches. These were the last shots fired over Anzac at the Turks. Then the flotilla turned its back on Gallipoli and swung slowly and sadly westward.

So ended the great 'get-away', a feat quite unparalleled in the annals of war. Historians will pay tribute to Sir Charles Monro and the Fleet.

We only take our hats off to General Birdwood and his staff and the staffs of the Australian divisions. But deep down we know the wonderful work our navy did during the eight months of the Gallipoli campaign. The army may make mistakes, but the navy is all right.

As we swing off, our last thought is not concerned with the bitterness of defeat. We think of our comrades quietly sleeping on Anzac. They gave their lives gladly, proudly, for Australia and the Empire. They showed the world that Australians could live and fight and die like Britishers.

There are many sad hearts on the transports tonight. And there are very many breaking hearts back in dear Australia. But old England has showered so many good gifts on her Colonies. The Colonies will not grudge this sacrifice for Empire.

LAST TO LEAVE

W. GAMBLE

On the eve of evacuating Anzac sixty men were selected to man the firing line and cover the retreat of the battalion. Ivor and I were included and held one post together. We mounted duty at 4 p.m. on the nineteenth and kept observing and sniping continually for almost a full round of the clock.

About 12 p.m. it was reported that all was going well on the beach and the next three hours seemed like an age. I thought the time would never come but, about 3 a.m., the word was passed quietly along and we sneaked through the tunnels (with about six layers of blankets wrapped around our feet), out into the open, down the winding saps to the beach, onto the lighter and away, without halting for one moment. It was a wonderful piece of work, wonderfully carried out to the smallest detail, even to marking our tracks by a trail of flour and salt, so that we would not lose our way in the dark.

ANZAC

'ARGENT'

Ah, well! We're gone! We're out of it now. We've something else to do.
But we all look back from the transport deck to the land-line far
    and blue:
Shore and valley are faded; fading are cliff and hill;
The land-line we called 'Anzac' . . . and we'll call it 'Anzac' still!
This last six months, I reckon, it'll be most of my life to me:
Trenches, and shells, and snipers, and the morning light on the sea,
Thirst in the broiling midday, shouts and gasping cries,
Big guns' talk from the water, and . . . flies, flies, flies, flies, flies!
And all of our trouble wasted! All of it gone for nix!
Still . . . we kept our end up—and some of the story sticks.
Fifty years on in Sydney they'll talk of our first big fight,
And even in little old, blind old England possibly someone might.
But seeing we had to clear, for we couldn't get on no more,
I wish that, instead of last night, it had been the night before.
Yesterday poor Jim stopped one. Three of us buried Jim.
I know a woman in Sydney that thought the world of him.
She was his mother. I'll tell her—broken with grief and pride—
'Mother' was Jim's last whisper. That was all. And he died.
Brightest and bravest and best of all—none could help but to
    love him—
And now . . . he lies there under the hill, with a wooden cross
    above him.
That's where it gets me twisted. The rest of it I don't mind,
But it don't seem right for me to be off, and to leave old Jim behind.
Jim, just quietly sleeping; and hundreds and thousands more;

For graves and crosses are mighty thick from Quinn's Post down to
    the shore!
Better there than in France, though, with the Germans' dirty work:
I reckon the Turk respects us, as we respect the Turk;
Abdul's a good, clean fighter, we've fought him, and we know,
And we've left him a letter behind us to tell him we found him so.
Not just to say, precisely, 'Goodbye' but 'Au revoir'!
Somewhere or other we'll meet again, before the end of the war!
But I hope it'll be a wider place, with a lot more room on the map,
And the airmen over the fight that day'll see a bit of a scrap!
Meanwhile, here's health to the Navy, that took us there, and away;
Lord! They're miracle-workers—and fresh ones every day!
My word! Those Mids in the cutters! Aren't they properly keen!
Don't ever say England's rotten—or not to us, who've seen!
Well! We're gone. We're out of it all! We've somewhere else to fight.
And we strain our eyes from the transport deck, but 'Anzac' is out
    of sight!
Valley and shore are vanished; vanished are cliff and hill;
And we may never go back to 'Anzac' . . . But I think that some of
    us will!

THE AFTERMATH

Gallipoli established the fighting reputation of the Anzacs and passed into Australian legend.

A total of 5482 Australian soldiers were killed in action during the Gallipoli campaign. A further 2012 soldiers died of wounds and 665 died from disease, bringing Australian battle losses to 8159. In all, 19,441 Australian soldiers were wounded. A total of 2721 New Zealanders were killed and 4752 were wounded.

Figures for the British were 21,255 dead and 52,230 wounded casualties. The French count wasn't accurate but was approximately 10,000 dead and 17,000 wounded.

Ottoman losses were 86,692 dead, 164,617 wounded and 20,000 who died from disease.

We have no accurate record of the numbers on the Allied side who died from disease but about 150 a day were evacuated with illness from June onwards.

It is safe to say over 150,000 men died during the Gallipoli campaign and twice that number were wounded. As the objective of the campaign was not realised, it was a futile exercise for the Allies. Ottoman army casualties were around a quarter of a million men either killed, wounded or lost through sickness. They eventually lost the war as well.

As far as the public importance of Anzac is concerned, it seems fairly obvious to me that two things created the iconic 'baptism of fire' that is so often talked about as part of our national identity.

The first of these was the 'chance' military decision made to combine the Aussie and Kiwi troops camped in Egypt into a separate fighting force, rather than spread the men out amongst British units. Secondly, there was the fact that we were a young nation with no military history of our own in world terms.

The 'Anzac spirit' is a palpable and wonderful truth that permeates our national character and gives us a real and justified sense of pride in our own unique national identity.

THE LETTERS OF THE DEAD

EDWARD DYSON

A letter came from Dick to-day;
A greeting glad he sent to me.
He tells of one more bloody fray—
Of how with bomb and rifle they
Have put their mark for all to see
Across rock-ribbed Gallipoli.

'How are you doing? Hope all's well,
I'm in great nick, and like the work.
Though there may be a brimstone smell,
And other pungent hints of Hell,
Not Satan's self can make us shirk
Our task of hitting up the Turk.

'He fights and falls, and comes again,
And knocks our charging lines about.
He's game at heart, and tough in grain,
And canters through the leaded rain,
Chock full of mettle—not a doubt
'Twill do us proud to put him out.

'But that's our job; to see it through
We've made our minds up, come what may,
This noon we had our work to do.
The shells were dropping two by two;
We fairly felt their bullets play
Among our hair for half a day.

'One clipped my ear, a red-hot kiss,
Another beggar chipped my shin.
They pass you with a vicious hiss
That makes you duck; but, hit or miss,
It isn't in the Sultan's skin
To shift Australia's cheerful grin.

'Soon homeward tramping with the band,
All notched a bit, and with the prize
Of glory for our native land,
I'll see my little sweetheart stand
And smile, her smile, so sweet and wise—
With proud tears shining in her eyes.'

A mist is o'er the written line
Whence martial ardor seems to flow;
A dull ache holds this heart of mine—
Poor boy, he had a vision fine;
But grave dust clouds the royal glow;
He died in action weeks ago!

He was my friend—I may not weep.
My soul goes out to Him who bled;
I pray for Christ's compassion deep
On mothers, lovers—all who keep
The woeful vigil, having read
The joyous letters of the dead.

AT RANDWICK HOSPITAL

ANONYMOUS—AN ARTICLE IN *THE SUN*, SYDNEY, 1917

It is Randwick Hospital, Sydney.

'Allow me to introduce Pte. Donnelly, 1st Battalion, commonly known as "Glutton", on account of having tried to eat a machine-gun,' says the man in pyjamas and overcoat.

'Couldn't swallow it,' laughs Pte. Donnelly, bringing his wheelchair to a standstill.

You are a trifle bewildered, and want to know more. 'Let us hear about it,' you ask.

'I'm afraid I've forgotten everything since I had shell-shock,' comes from the wheelchair.

'He's stringing you!' the other convalescent protests. 'Go on, Donnelly; be a sport!'

'Did you really suffer from shell-shock?' demands the visitor.

'Yes, from eating peanuts!' says the incorrigible one; but a few more protests set him on the narrow pathway of truth, and you learn that after four months on Gallipoli he got so badly peppered by a machine-gun that his mates suspected him of having tried to eat it.

He was taken off to Malta with a complement of thirty-two bullets. He marks off the joint of his first finger to show the length of them. His right arm is of use only when lifted in a certain way, and it will be a week or two yet before he is able to discard the wheelchair. His legs show several crevices where bullets entered.

'I'll have to wear stockings in surf-bathing now,' he says whimsically, and with eyes too rueful to be anything but comic. 'This was a bull's-eye,' he continues, opening his tunic so that you can see a cup-shaped wound in his chest. The bullet came out through the shoulder.

During the Gallipoli campaign Pte. Donnelly went from a Friday afternoon until the following Tuesday with five hours' sleep. 'In action,' he says, 'you never feel tired, even when you've been at it for as long as three or four days; but as soon as you come off duty you go flop.

'I remember being sent into the trenches. There were regular rooms where you could lie down. They were shell-proof, and, as you may imagine, very dim. I went along the trench looking for a place to rest, and I met one of my pals. "Oh," he said, "the big room along here is all right. I'll wake you when your time's up."

'I stumbled along, and when I got there the place was full except for one bit of floor just big enough for me. I tiptoed over the others to it, and lay down, with my water bottle for a pillow. There were two big chaps either side of me, and as they'd been there before me I took it they'd had a pretty fair innings, so made myself more comfortable by shoving one of them against the wall. My pal woke me at 9 p.m. I asked him for a cigarette, and when I struck the match I said to him, "My word, those fellows are doing well, sleeping so long."

'He laughed, and I took another look at them. I had been sleeping between two dead Turks! But you didn't take any notice of things like that out there!

'On the day of the armistice I and two others were at a part of the lines known as the Chamber of Horrors. It was the unfinished section of what we hoped would eventually join up with Quinn's Post. There was only room for three in it, and it was quite close to the German officers' quarters in the enemy trenches. The enemy did not know that, though, and we had strict orders not to betray the unfinished state of the lines, as had they charged us there we should have had no place of retreat but the tunnel which was being gradually made with the idea of joining up.

'One of the three suggested taking a peep over on this day. I did so very cautiously, and, to my surprise, saw a big German officer in his shirt sleeves advancing with a white flag. I told the others. But this time more were advancing. One of the boys in the Chamber of Horrors thought that at least this section of the enemy was surrendering. He leapt up on the parapet, shouting, "Good for you, matey! Are you going to quit? Come and shake hands with us." He was dragged down, and the news of the armistice soon passed along to us.

'The quietness of those few hours was almost more than we could bear after continual firing. If a man spoke to you, you jumped at the sound of his voice. It was uncanny the way all the little singing birds came back as soon as it was quiet. The whole thing got on our nerves, and we were glad when the time came for the armistice to end.

'The Turks had the right to start off again, and I never heard anything so puny as the first shot that was fired. Then the old naval guns got to it, and we were happy again.

'During the armistice I made friends with a Turk. He spoke perfect English. He had been coming out to Sydney to join his uncle and nephew in business, but five days before his departure he was called up. We exchanged cigarettes—I gave him a box of those awful Scotch things we used to get out there, and he gave me the real Turkish article, which, I can tell you, I enjoyed.

'While we smoked he said, "Strange, you know! Today we smoke, chat, and are happy together; tomorrow we shall probably pour lead into each other!" He was taken prisoner afterwards, and I saw him again. He was a really good fellow, like many of the other rural Turks against whom we fought.

'Life in the trenches? Well, there wasn't any dinner bell! We took bully beef and biscuits with us, and opened the beef whenever we were hungry and had the chance of eating.

'There was one fellow who had been a shearer's cook. He made a sort of grater by piercing a piece of tin with holes. He used to grate the biscuits and beef, and make rissoles and cutlets and things. My word, we wouldn't have lost him for a fortune. We were the envy of the lines.

'One day someone shot a hare (the first and last I saw on the peninsula). It was a lord mayor's banquet! We grilled it, and as soon as a bit was cooked it would be hacked off, and it was "Goodbye, hare".

***

Pte. Donnelly was in London for Anzac Day. He says that most of the Australians had fresh tunics made for the occasion, more smartly cut than usual. He and several others were in a theatre during the day. In the seat in front was a broad-shouldered Australian in khaki. They recognised him as a pal.

'How bout it, Nugget?' said one of the soldiers, laying his hand on the shoulder of the Anzac in front. 'Nugget' turned round, and, to their dismay, they saw the crown of a General on his shoulder. 'Beg pardon, sir,' said they; 'thought you were one of ourselves.'

'Well, damn it all, aren't I?' said the General. 'Come out and have a drink.'

He refused to tell them his name, and they have never discovered it.

KILLED IN ACTION

HARRY McCANN

Where the ranges throw their shadows long before the day's surrender,
Down a valley where a river used to tumble to the sea,
On a rising patch of level rest the men who dared to tender
Life and all its sweetness for their love o' liberty.

In a thousand miles of ugly scrubby waste and desolation,
Just that little space of level showing open to the sea;
Nothing here to lend it grandeur (sure, it needs no decoration)
Save those rows of wooden crosses keeping silent custody.

There's a band of quiet workers, artless lads who joked and chatted
Just this morning; now they're sullen and they keep their eyes away
From the blanket-hidden body, coat and shirt all blood-bespattered,
Lying motionless and waiting by the new-turned heap of clay.

There are records in the office—date of death and facts pertaining,
Showing name and rank and number and disposal of the kit—
More or less a business matter, and we have no time for feigning
More than momentary pity for the men who have been hit.

There's a patient mother gazing on her hopes so surely shattered
(Hopes and prayers she cherished bravely, seeking strength to hide
    her fear),
Boyhood's dreams and idle memories—things that never really
    mattered—
Lying buried where he's buried 'neath the stars all shining clear.

There's a young wife sorrow-stricken in her bitter first conception
Of that brief conclusive message, harsh fulfilment of her dread;
There are tiny lips repeating, with their childish imperception,
Simple words that bring her mem'ries from the boundaries of
    the dead.

Could the Turk have seen this picture when his trigger-finger
    rounded?
Would his sights have blurred a little had he heard that mother's
    prayer?
Could he know some things that she knew, might his hate have
    been confounded?
But he only saw his duty, and he did it, fighting fair.

Just a barren little surface where the grave mounds rise ungainly,
Monuments and tributes to the men who've done their share.
Pain and death, the fruits of battle, and the crosses tell it plainly,
Short and quick and silent suffering; would to God it ended there.

A STRANGE BOND

JIM HAYNES

In October 2004 Ali Salih Dirik and I stood at Anzac Cove and catalogued the similarities between the Turkish and Australian experiences on the peninsula in 1915:

- Both nations were involved in a war of someone else's making.
- The Turkish troops at Gallipoli were fighting as part of a larger force, the Ottoman army, under German command. Australian troops were part of the Anzac force, under British command. Both Turks and Australians were part of larger force.
- The Ottoman army was a part of the Central Powers' forces. The Anzac divisions were a small part of the Allied forces.
- Turkish and Australasian troops displayed courage well beyond the call of duty.
- Both Turks and Anzacs respected each other as men of honour and decency.
- The campaign would become, for both nations, a defining moment in their national history. What happened in those eight months would become an essential element in each nation's heritage and a symbol of their national character, pride and independence.

For both Australia and New Zealand, the Gallipoli campaign was the event that would stamp them as independent nations, both at war and in more general terms on the world stage. Even more significant, perhaps, was the effect the campaign had at home on the self-perception of both nations as independent entities with their own unique characteristics which were reflected in the character of their fighting force.

The Anzacs represented a breed of men whose character, appearance, speech and attitude to life differed from that of their British ancestors and the other British troops at Gallipoli—and it is amazing to think that it was only a chance organisational move, a decision made while the troops were encamped in Egypt, that saw the Australian and New Zealand troops even fight as discrete, combined entity. They could have easily been spread throughout the other British forces as they had been in South Africa.

The way the forces were organised at Gallipoli actually made it possible for the Anzacs to be seen as separate from the other British forces. Thus their differences and characteristics were able to be perceived by all and sundry, including their allies, their enemies and those at home.

For the modern Turkish nation, the events surrounding the Gallipoli campaign represent significant milestones on the path to emerging Turkish nationalism. The Ottoman Empire was crumbling and the Turkish nation would rise like a phoenix from its ashes.

There are three elements that, in retrospect, make the Gallipoli campaign a very Turkish victory, rather than an Ottoman one: the defeat of the British and French fleet at the Narrows on 18 March 1915; the holding of the peninsula against the three-pronged Allied invasion at Helles, Anzac Cove and Suvla Bay; and the fact that Turkey's greatest national hero, Kemal Ataturk, rose to fame as a result of his involvement at Gallipoli.

Turks refer to the Gallipoli campaign as 'The Battle of Canakkale' and the significant date for them is 18 March, not 25 April. This was the day the British and French fleet was defeated and turned back from its attempt to force the Straits by Turkish guns, mines and torpedoes. As a national day in Turkey, 18 March is a celebration of Turkish nationhood—not a celebration of an old Ottoman victory.

The holding of the peninsula against the Allied forces is also generally seen by Turks as one of the first acts of a Turkish nation. Yet Turks made up only a part of the Ottoman army, just as

Anzacs made up only a part of the Allied army. In fact, two-thirds of the Ottoman forces on 25 April at Gallipoli were made up of Arab regiments, not Turkish ones.

For Turks, perhaps the most important element of the campaign is that it saw the emergence of their greatest national hero and the father of their nation, Mustafa Kemal, later known as Kemal Ataturk. Ataturk was elected Turkey's first president and instituted sweeping social changes and reforms.

When you begin to consider these elements of the Gallipoli experience, the seemingly strange bond between old enemies becomes a little easier to fathom.

What Anzac means to us as a nation today, I don't really know. When I read the accounts that make up this book I am in awe of the men who wrote them and fought in that campaign. I don't think we 'make 'em like that anymore', but perhaps we can find something in the Anzac legend to make us all better citizens and better people.

THE SOUL OF THE ANZAC

RODERIC QUINN

The form that was mine was brown and hard,
And thewed and muscled, and tall and straight;
And often it rode from the straight yard,
And often it passed through the stockyard gate;
And often it paused on the grey skyline
'Twixt mulga and mallee or gum and pine.

There was never a task that it would not do;
There was never a labour it left undone;
But ever and always it battled through,
And took the rest that its toil had won,
And slept the sleep of the weary-limbed
Till the stars grew pale and the planets dimmed.

The form that was mine is mine no more,
For low it lies in a soldier's grave
By an alien sea on an alien shore;
And over its sleep no wattles wave
And stars unseen on their journey creep;
But it wakes no more from its dreamless sleep.

O mother of mine, what is is best!
And our graves are dug at the hour of birth;
And the form that slept on your shielding breast
Sleeps soundly here in the mothering earth.
And dust to dust! When our part is played,
Does it matter much where the change is made?

O Heart that was mind, you were brave and strong—
How strong, how brave, let another tell!
You love the lilt of the bushman's song,
And loved the land that he loved so well,
And loved—ah, well!—as well as she knew,
The sweet, white girl who was all to you.

O Heart of mine, though your love was great,
Yet another greater than Love is lord of man;
The rose-path wound to The Peaks began;
And though the storm threatened and skies grew black,
You dared the menace and took the track.

O Heart, when the cliffs were hard to climb,
How sweet was home, and her eyes so sweet!
How sweet the moments when Love kept time,
And you and her heart gave beat for beat,
And waters sang, and the sun-rays glanced,
And the flowers laughed out, and the saplings danced.

Yet better, O Heart, to do as you did
Than to lie on her breast, as your love-gift lies;
For how can Love prosper when Honour lies hid,
Ashamed to look Love fair and square in the eyes?
Though grave-mould be round you, grey grasses above,
You live, and shall live, evermore in her love!

O Man that I was, you were foe to Death;
For Life was fair to you—wonderful, rare;
You had your being and drew your breath
In ample spaced of earth and air;
While ever and always, by night and day,
Bright Promise pointed the Golden Way.

And yet 'twas your choice to be this thing—
A young man dead on an alien shore,
Where the immemorial surges sing
As once they sang in the days of yore,
When Greek and Trojan matched their might
And Troy shone down upon the fight.

O Man that I was, well done! Well done!
You chose the nobler, the better part;
Though a mother weep for her soldier son,
And a fair, sweet girl be sad at heart,
Yet the soul of your country glows with pride
At the deed you did and the death you died!

THE ENIGMATIC
MR BLOCKSIDGE

JIM HAYNES

By far the most enigmatic of the authors included in this volume is William Baylebridge. Born Charles William Blocksidge in 1883, the son of a Brisbane auctioneer and estate agent, he was educated at Brisbane Grammar School and had the classical scholar David Owen as a private tutor.

In 1908 Blocksidge went to London, determined, it seems, to become a poet. In London he self-published several volumes of poetry, copies of which were sent to the principal public libraries, but hardly any were sold to the public. He changed his name to William Baylebridge some time after 1923, and during his life wrote stories, philosophy, and much poetry.

Baylebridge returned to Queensland in 1919 after travelling extensively in Europe, Egypt and the Middle East. He is said to have been involved in 'special literary work' during the war and his familiarity with his subject material in *An Anzac Muster* certainly suggests that he had personal experience at the front. There is no evidence, however, to show that he belonged to any of the fighting forces.

Both in his literary and private life Baylebridge was intriguing. A tall, good-looking man, he was a strong athlete and musician with an interest in the stock exchange. There is no suggestion of eccentricity, yet, while he was anxious for literary recognition, he adopted methods of publication which made this impossible. He was continually revising and rewriting his earlier work and always self-published his efforts in very small editions.

Some considered his work to be profound, innovative and unique, while others found it just plain dreadful. A review in *The Bulletin* in 1912 called him 'a new prophet, a new poet . . . or a new lunatic' and described his verse as 'astonishing in its gassy rhetoric and its foolishness'. In 1930, however, literary critic H.A. Kellow hailed Baylebridge as 'the greatest literary figure that Queensland has yet produced', and a 1939 collected edition of his earlier poems, *This Vital Flesh*, was awarded the Australian Literature Society's gold medal for the most important volume of Australian poetry of its year.

An Anzac Muster was written in a very oddly stylised literary fashion to replicate Chaucer's *Canterbury Tales* and was issued in an edition of one hundred copies that are now exceedingly rare. Baylebridge never married and lived the last twenty years of his life in Sydney, where he died in 1942.

A DREAM OF ANZAC

WILLIAM BAYLEBRIDGE

This story is a fictional account of a soldier's dream, which weirdly predicts how Australians would feel about Anzac decades after it occurred. Strangely it was written during the event and assumes that the Turks would be defeated, yet it predicts with eerie prescience the way we celebrate the Gallipoli campaign a century later.

***

By 8 August the gallant 29th Division had pushed well into the containing battle at Krithia. At Lone Pine the 1st Brigade of Australian Infantry had taken the Turkish positions, and the New Zealanders, the right covering column of the main attack, had charged and secured the almost impregnable old No. 3 Post.

The gullies, won at a bitter price in blood, were open to the two attacking columns which, even now, were advancing to the assault.

The Turks, threatened as they had never expected to be, put forth their entire strength to cut us off from the crests that meant final victory. Their reserves were brought up in great numbers to meet this threat which, had the odds not been insuperable, would have meant an end to their hopes.

The men of our right attacking column, paying with their lives for every foot of territory won, toiled up the gullies and formed a rough line up past the Table Top. Then they threw themselves into the confused struggle, which led on towards the stubborn heights of Chunuk Bair.

Our remaining column, the Australians and their comrades on the left, laboured up the crags and across the chasms of the Aghyl Dere. They had set their hearts on attaining the high ultimate goal—Koja Chemen Tepe. This peak, dominating the whole peninsula, was the key to make victory ours.

In this last column there was a Queenslander named McCullough. Because he was much given to dreaming queer dreams, men called him the Prophet. But, though his strange dreams and premonitions had run to many new and strange things, none were as strange as this delirious dream he was living now. To any sane man this advance seemed to be the nightmare of a madman.

With their blood up, and with a will that was more than human urging them on, these men struggled forward, cursing, killing, almost drowning in the billowing smoke and dust spread by exploding shells. Great masses of earth were torn away and entombed them. Men were spattered with the bowels and brains of comrades. The hungry wire raked at their flesh, and was left dripping with their blood. Bombs and bayonets dispersed them on the shaking earth.

Night turned to the agony of dawn, and day to night again, and those who were not dead still moved on. Many would think that those who had been left in the scrub below, now just shapes without human meaning, were the lucky ones, for they had done with all this agony.

And in the shambles down there—one of those countless uncommemorated souls—lay Pat McCullough. He had struggled on with that marvellous company of men till he was exhausted from his wounds, his sight had become confused and his senses had lost their reckoning. Then he had dropped in a limp heap beside that track, a track watered with the blood and sweat that shall give it significance, and sanctify it, to Australians forever.

***

When McCullough woke, he found himself among boulders in a small depression, shut in with scrub. He stretched himself, rubbed his eyes, yawned, and sat up. The air was clear, and almost without sound. There was some touch of freshness that told him it was still early in the day. Nothing looked amiss—a pair of doves sat preening each other on a fir bush. Up aloft an intent hawk cut lessening circles against a background of pale blue as if he had sighted some business in the neighbourhood.

'Strange!' thought McCullough. 'How did I get here?'

He scrambled to his feet, took a few steps into the undergrowth, and discovered that the ground about him was the summit of an insignificant hill.

In a flash all that he had been through came back to him—all that had happened before this awakening—that mad scramble to death or victory up the blood-sodden gullies.

But what was this?

Pressing his hand to his forehead, as if to help his memory, he gazed about in an effort to understand. The place looked, he thought, like the discarded pit some artillery battery had used.

'Strange!' he repeated.

What struck him was the weird stillness of the place. The roar of our guns, the heavy rumbling of far-off howitzers, the bursting of shells, the vicious snap of rifles, the shouting of men on the beach, the human noise of men cursing, or singing at their work, or crunching along hard roads were all gone. The thousand sounds of war that once echoed through these hills might never have been.

It was so quiet. What did this mean?

And then, in a flash of perception, a reason came.

Deaf! Of course, he was deaf. Had he not been partially deaf many times before from the artillery and shrapnel? His hearing had gone now for good.

Yet, even as he asserted this, he knew that he was not deaf. A fitful morning was blowing in from the sea, flapping the leaves of a shrub nearby. That, beyond question, he heard. Yes, and he also heard, up in the silent air, a lark singing; and there were pigeons, in the scrub below, making an audible job of their wooing.

'Surely,' he thought, 'I am still Pat McCullough, and this is Anzac; but, if that's so, my wits are totally out somewhere.'

There was plainly need for some tough thinking; and selecting a spot for this, he sat down to do it. He felt his limbs, gingerly, with trepidation. They were as solid as a rail—the scarred but substantial flesh and bone of a soldier—and none, thank God, missing!

Then it struck him that he had no clothes on: he was bare. In the same breath he felt a queer tickling on his belly and found that a great bunch of hair had set up the titillation.

'What's this?' he began and then, breaking off, stroked his chin and burst suddenly into a laugh.

'A beard!' he exclaimed. 'Verily,' he laughed, 'the Prophet hath his beard!'

So grotesque did this transformation seem to McCullough that he questioned his very identity. Had he died down there in the gully? Was this mystery to be explained by the transmigration of souls? Had he left his former flesh and gone, by some dark process, into a different body?

It flashed on him, at this point, that he could clear up this question easily.

He felt under his left breast. The old scar was still there! Another piece of shrapnel, he remembered, had knocked two teeth away on the right half of his jaw. He put his hand up, and found the gap.

He brought to mind other marks, marks that had cost the foe something—and these he went through carefully till he was convinced he was McCullough. This was his skin, and the same bone, and the hair—at least some of it—that had gone shearing with him from Carpentaria to down below Bourke.

Having settled this point, he breathed easier.

The next question to clear up was the identity of the place. Though the soil and the scrub were certainly just as at Anzac, this silence was uncanny. It was entirely out of keeping with the stir and ear-shaking noises that never stopped on the battlefield.

McCullough got up, and made for a little spur which, as he expected, commanded a good view of the country round about. He pushed carefully through the gorse, taking great care to protect his bare flesh, and came out onto a crumbling pinnacle, running almost sheer to the ravine below.

The land beyond this ravine was fairly flat; it was patched with crops, and carried groves of grey-leafed olive trees. This part he did not know well; but that hill in the distance, that stubborn-looking lump on the skyline, was surely Achi Baba, a hill of many memories.

To McCullough, the weightiest thing in life now was to make sure.

Picking his way to another spur, he looked hard and long. Before him, now, lay a confused mass of broken hills. McCullough rubbed his eyes. Surely he knew that landscape, and that peak! Hell and death, he ought to! But what was that great, imposing mass, stuck there on the top of it?

The peak should be Koja Chemen; but the building, or whatever it was, that caught the rays of the ascending sun on its bright surface, what was that? And what were these other marks—that looked so odd here—these structures (if they were indeed that) which had cropped up where, until now, only snipers had crawled?

Was it Anzac, and yet not Anzac? Or was he mad? Or was this dreaming?

Noting the position of the sun he pushed over to that side of the hill which, if the place was still what it had been, must look out to the Aegean Sea.

What he should see there would fix it. There would lie the swarm of multi-shaped barges, laden with munitions for both guns and men, and longboats, lined with the wounded, would be putting out in tow to the hospital ships. The fidgety destroyers and the battle-ships would be there, and the bones of wrecked shipping, too.

A few steps now, and one glance would decide it. He would soon know how his case stood, for the scene was as well known to him as his own home. Hurried forward by these thoughts, he shoved his way through the brush, and stood breathless on the hill's edge.

If McCullough had found marvels before, now there was really something to gape at!

What could this mean?

There was the beach he had fought up in that ghostly dawn of the twenty-fifth. He knew every foot of that. There, before him, was the first ridge—heaped, when he had seen it last, with almost its own weight of stores, and honeycombed with dug-outs. But, there was no trace whatever now of those stores, and there, in the near distance, lay the scarps under which they had so recently fought that bitter fight, on the seventh, eighth and ninth of August . . . this August? . . . last August? . . . or what August?

His eye, still in quest of a solution to this riddle of the familiar and the unfamiliar, travelled back to the beach, curving around, in the shape of a boomerang, to Suvla.

It was the beach, positively, beyond doubt, where men had laughed, and cursed, and swum, and died. Ah, what soldier who had taken his baptism there could mistake it? The waves of the blue Aegean Sea broke gently upon it as they did often of old.

Yes, Anzac, it was Anzac in truth, it was; but yet not the Anzac it had been—not *his* Anzac.

For there he saw a pretentious pier, and a smug modern hotel was perched where the field hospital had once perched on the hill! A hotel it must be, surely. But for what? For whom?

There were also different trees, which looked well established. Many of them, in a blaze of gold, threw the perfect colour across the drab landscape before him. What trees were these?

As if to answer his question, the breeze carried up a perfume, which he sensed, with a sudden wonderment of delight. Wattle!

Well, that was something. The men there would at least sleep among their own trees, the trees they had slept among so often in their own land. But all these things that belonged to a world so remote, how did *they* get there?

To McCullough there was something about the whole business that was more than uncanny. It was as if he was living in two worlds, and was a lost soul in each.

God! If only he could but shake off the obsession of either world and struggle back somehow, as a complete and satisfied entity, to one of them—no matter which!

He saw what he saw; all the life of the place as he had known it, from the beach to the top trenches, had disappeared. But why should it? That strip of shore, where men had loafed, or hauled guns and lumber to land, or shouldered ammunition, and beef, and biscuit or waited their turn for water, had become his whole existence.

These things were no longer on the shore. They had given place to this—the antithesis of all that had been there formerly. But why? How?

McCullough could make nothing of it.

So absorbed was he in all of this, trying to save his wits from a collapse, that he did not hear the footsteps of a stranger who just now arrived, after a stiff climb, at the summit of the hill. The newcomer, mopping his forehead, and peering in all directions as he did so, saw McCullough half-hidden in the scrub.

'Seen a platoon of turkeys about here, mate?' he called out.

McCullough turned sharply and there, looking human enough, was the shape which had addressed this question to him. He came out of the scrub and confronted a stout fellow, very red in the face, attired in shorts, and carrying a shot-gun.

Both men stared in surprise. McCullough, clothed as Adam had been, gave the newcomer a queer sensation about the spine. The gentleman held his gun ready for emergencies.

'Seen some turkeys about here, mate?' he repeated, edging off a little.

McCullough found no words to reply with. His ideas got confused again. If this fellow was looking for the enemy with a weapon no better than that in his fist, he was mad.

'They're the best table birds the boss has,' the man went on, evidently confused too, and feeling himself under the necessity of saying something. 'And he'll want them soon. Sure you haven't seen them?'

'I'm a stranger here,' answered McCullough, swallowing a lump which, for some reason, came into his throat.

'How'd you get here? And where's your gear?'

'The truth is,' McCullough replied, scratching his head, 'that's just what I've been trying to find out.'

The man with the gun, though plainly a bit suspicious, could not question the doubt expressed in the face before him, for it was sincere enough. Men, he knew, could lose their memories; and in such cases anything was possible.

'You'd better hop down to the pub,' he said at last, 'and see what the boss'll do for you.'

'Then that building *is* a pub?'

'It is—the best on the peninsula.'

The best on the peninsula, thought McCullough. Then there must be others! He was again seized with a passionate desire to have a solution to this mystery.

'D'you know this place well?' McCullough questioned. The cloud of a few minutes back had already lifted magically from his spirit; and he felt a little of his old confidence again.

'Know it?' answered the man, with obvious pride. 'I know every turn and crack, every peak and precipice, of this patch—every foot of every trench, the ground of every engage-ment, of every victory—every boneyard I know too. If you want the history of this glorious battlefield,' he went on, with a flourish, 'I'm your man. That's my job. I'm a guide here.'

That puzzling construction on Koja Chemen, his companion explained, was a monument to commemorate the deeds of those who had fought, and those who had perished, on the peninsula. Housed in it, in a small temple, were the great books in which their names were recorded. This monument could be seen a long way off, and from all sides—it must have impressed, McCullough thought, the shipping of all nations in the Straits.

These records were the duplicates of similar records—housed also in a national temple—which were kept, for eternal remembrance, in the Australian capital. The peninsula, from Helles to the lines at Bulair, was British; and many thousands, Australians mostly, made pilgrimages to the place. Hence the large number of hotels and the guides for the battle-ground and all the paraphernalia for the use of sightseers.

Wattle had been planted and coaxed into growth, till the spot, in parts, looked a true piece of Australia. Military pundits had been busy there; and their many volumes, of many opinions, had been duly presented to the world. Every memory of that place, in short, was treasured as a national possession; and all existing records of the occupation were preserved as things sacred. These, and many other matters perhaps not so relevant, the man made plain to the astonished McCullough.

'And does Australia think so much of the job those fellows did here?' he asked, with a modesty lost on his companion.

The guide whipped out his book—for he always carried it—and, opening it with the skill that comes of much practice, he struck an attitude, and began an oration in this style:

'In these hills, on this holy ground, the sons of Australia, in deeds of the noblest heroism, achieved much in one of the greatest labours ever given to men. Here they fought and died in a way that shall grip the imagination, yes, and thrill the heart, so long as men walk upon this earth. Here they won that heritage which shall be prized, and not least by their own people, so long as nations are nations; for it was here that Australia first proved herself and became a nation. If all the great—'

'Hold hard!' McCullough interrupted. 'Got a smoke on you?'

The speechmaker, a little piqued at the interruption, felt in his pocket, produced a couple of cigarettes, and handed them over with some matches. He was about to return to his book when they heard the whistle of a steamer.

'Strike me!' said the late orator, thrusting the volume with haste into his coat, 'there's the *Australia Comes* putting in, full of tourists, I'd better look smart—guide business.'

At this the man's mind appeared to return suddenly to the present; and the incongruity before him—of this naked man. What could he do with him? The expected guests would have to be considered. At this juncture he could hardly take him to the hotel, clothed, as he was, only in whiskers.

'Hide yourself up here till I send some togs up,' he shouted, waving his hand; and he hurried off to be in place for the trade promised by the steamer's arrival.

McCullough pinched himself to make sure that he was thoroughly awake.

It seemed to him that he was thoroughly awake.

'So this's what it's come to!' he said to himself; and there was some bitterness in the reflection.

'Somehow I've lived long enough to see this. I've lived long enough to meet someone who knows this place better than the men did who made it . . . Well, he's had a better chance than we had.

'Or has he?' he went on, after a moment. 'After all, he'll never know it. Only those who were here in my time will do that. We had the substance; others have but the shadow—though no doubt they'll be the richer ones.

'This fellow's a parasite,' he said aloud, considering it further, 'or perhaps I'm all wrong. Perhaps there's some right thinking behind all this after all. The shadow may be more than the substance.

'But, by God,' he concluded, 'I'd like to run into some who did their bit here, and pass the joke on.'

The steamer whistled again; and McCullough pushed back through the scrub to the spur, which overlooked the beach. He saw a large vessel coming in under a good head of steam. Nearer and nearer she came—her decks alive with a freight very different from that carried in his time!

As he gazed, like one in a trance, the liner drew in cautiously to the pier; and the place, which before had seemed unpeopled, soon became crowded with men and women. Vehicles were making their way down to the landing place; and, guessing these to be the means of transit to the pub higher up, it struck McCullough that the dry throat must have been notably out of fashion in this later breed of Anzac.

It was a long time since McCullough had seen a crowd like that—in another existence, it seemed. There were men in holiday attire such as he had seen on the pier at Southport and women in clothes that were new and much changed in fashion since the casting-out of his soul into the wasteland . . . but very becoming, he thought, for all that.

There were youths, too, and girls of all ages.

McCullough felt a great longing to get closer to that crowd.

So strong was this feeling that he pushed further out upon the spur which, being eroded and sandy like much of the land there, gave way suddenly beneath his weight. He made a frantic attempt to get back to safety—but too late. With a swiftness that completely blotted out his senses, he dropped, amidst a great welter of stones and dust, into the ravine below.

***

'I think he'll do well enough now,' said the doctor, as he turned, with something like a smile, from the bed in the hospital ship. 'He seems to be recovering and I think he'll beat the fish this time.'

McCullough opened his eyes. He could feel a heavy wrapping of bandages about his head and limbs. Above him, looking down into his own, he saw a woman's face, a nurse's face.

'So you've stopped dreaming at last?' she said.

LEON GELLERT

JIM HAYNES

Leon Gellert was a poet, soldier and respected journalist and newspaperman. Born in 1892 and educated in Adelaide, he was beaten by his father until he decided to take self-defence lessons at the YMCA and threw his father on his back when he was next attacked.

Gellert left school at seventeen, worked as a pupil-teacher at Unley Public School and, with the financial help of an uncle, educated himself further at Adelaide University and taught P.E. at Hindmarsh Public School until he enlisted as a private in the AIF in October 1914.

Gellert landed on Anzac Beach at dawn on 25 April and survived nine weeks on Gallipoli before being wounded by shrapnel and suffering from septicaemia and dysentery. He had to be evacuated to Malta, where he contracted typhoid and was sent to England to convalesce. That is where most of his Anzac poems, later collected together in *Songs of a Campaign*, were written.

After collapsing into a coma Gellert was diagnosed as having epilepsy, repatriated and discharged as medically unfit in June 1916. Amazingly, he re-enlisted in Adelaide in November, only to be discharged four days later when his medical record was uncovered.

He returned to teaching, at Norwood Public School, and revised and added to *Songs of a Campaign*, which was hailed by *The Bulletin* as one of the best verse collections to have come out of the war. Published in 1917, the book won the prestigious Bundey prize for English verse, and in 1918 Angus & Robertson

Ltd published a third and enlarged edition, illustrated by Norman Lindsay.

A second collection of verse, *The Isle of San*, was published as a limited edition in 1919, but Gellert became disillusioned with literature and turned to journalism.

After his marriage to Kathleen Saunders on Christmas Day 1918, the couple moved to Sydney where Gellert taught English at Cleveland Street Intermediate High School until 1922. He wrote a column for *Smith's Weekly* and, through his friendship with Norman Lindsay, became editor of *Art in Australia* and a director of Art in Australia Ltd, which also published the magazine *Home* that Gellert edited as well.

This led to other editing positions and he continued working in Sydney as a journalist and literary editor with *The Daily Telegraph* and *The Sydney Morning Herald* until his wife died in 1969.

Gellert then returned to Adelaide and spent his last years with his pet dachshund at Hazelwood Park in a house he called Crumble Cottage. He died in August 1977.

Leon Gellert was a great character and a truly gifted poet. His Anzac poetry and children's verse were much anthologised and remembered throughout the first half of the twentieth century, but are now mostly long out of print and forgotten.

ANZAC COVE

LEON GELLERT

There's a lonely stretch of hillocks;
There's a beach asleep and drear;
There's a battered broken fort beside the sea.
There are sunken, trampled graves;
And a little rotting pier;
And winding paths that wind unceasingly.
There's a torn and silent valley;
There's a tiny rivulet
With some blood upon the stones beside its mouth.
There are lines of buried bones;
There's an unpaid waiting debt;
There's a sound of gentle sobbing in the South.

OUR SONS AS WELL

JIM HAYNES

These days Turkey is still a poor nation by European standards. Many Turks have migrated over the past decades—one and a half million, in fact. The bulk of these have relocated on a temporary basis as 'migrant workers' in European nations, especially Germany.

Turkish migration to Australia, however, has for the most part been by families wanting to settle permanently. Government-assisted migration to Australia began in 1968 and the early intake was of unskilled labourers and peasant families with little English. Since the 1980s this has changed and permanent visas are given only to highly skilled Turks and those qualifying under family reunion regulations. According to the 2006 census, there were some 59,400 Turkish Australians.

***

In 1972 a Turkish migrant and former Turkish heavyweight wrestling champion, Kemal Dover, decided to march with six other Turks in Sydney's Anzac Day march under a banner that read 'Turkish–Australian Friendship Will Never Die'. Their participation was apparently completely unofficial but well received by the crowd.

When official requests were made by Turkish groups to be involved in Anzac Day in the early 1980s, they were denied. Victorian RSL president Bruce Ruxton famously stated, 'Anyone that was shooting us doesn't get in.'

The Turkish attitude to their old foe, the Anzacs, has always been generous, forgiving and understanding. When our official Australian War Historian, Charles Bean, returned to the peninsula in 1919 to document and photograph the battlefields and the graves, he was received with courtesy and respect. Similar cooperation was afforded to the Commonwealth War Graves Commission, which was assisted by the Turks in setting up the many beautifully laid-out and cared-for Allied graveyards on the peninsula.

Even though the Ottoman army lost more than 86,000 men at Gallipoli, compared to 11,000 Anzacs and 31,000 British and French, there is really only one Ottoman cemetery on the peninsula. It is a combined cemetery, mosque and memorial to the 57th Regiment. It contains a wall showing 1,817 names of those who died from the regiment.

The 57th was one of those under the command of Kemal Ataturk. An all-Turkish regiment, it happened to be on the parade ground ready for exercises when news of the landing came on the morning of 25 April. It was the regiment to which Kemal issued the famous order-of-the-day:

> I don't order you to attack, I order you to die. In the time it takes us to die, other troops and commanders can come and take our places.

In buying time to allow reinforcements to be brought up into place on 25 April, the 57th Regiment was completely wiped out.

The Turks did build other monuments at various places on the battlefields at Anzac and at Helles. There is a gigantic statue of Kemal Ataturk on the spot where he turned the tide of the battle at Chunuk Bair. It stands beside the enormous monolithic memorial to the New Zealanders who died defending the hill.

There are a few isolated Turkish graves and other Turkish memorials and statues on the peninsula, including the statue of a brave Turkish soldier who carried a wounded British officer back to his trench during the fighting on 25 April. The bulk of the memorials and graveyards, however, are those of the invaders, not the defenders.

In 1934 Kemal Ataturk summed up many Turks' sentiments about the experience of 1915 when he wrote the words now enshrined on an enormous cement tablet above Anzac Cove:

To those heroes that shed their blood and lost their lives . . .

You are now lying in the soil of a friendly country, therefore rest in peace.

There is no difference between the Johnnies and the Mehemets to us where they lie side by side here in this country of ours.

You, the mothers who sent your sons from far away countries . . .

Wipe away your tears; your sons are now lying in our bosom and are in peace. After having lost their lives on this land they have become our sons as well.

***

In 1973 the Turkish government designated 330 square kilometres of the peninsula as the Gallipoli Peninsula National Historical Park. In 1997 this became a Peace Park with a rehabilitation plan organised by the International Union of Architects.

From the late 1980s there has been Turkish representation in Anzac Day marches in Australia and, in 1985, a small group of Anzac veterans returned to Gallipoli on Anzac Day as invited guests of the Turkish government. At the same time Turkey officially renamed Ari Burnu Cove 'Anzac Cove', or 'Anzak Koyu' in Turkish.

A larger group of Gallipoli veterans was there for the dawn service in 1990 to mark the seventy-fifth anniversary of Anzac Day, along with 10,000 others, including then Australian prime minister, Bob Hawke, and political leaders from Turkey, New Zealand and the United Kingdom.

Since that time the pilgrimage to Gallipoli for Anzac Day has grown to the point where new roads are having to be built to deal with the convoys of buses bringing in more than 20,000 travellers each Anzac Day. The centenary celebrations have been planned for years.

What is even more significant is that the crowd consists, to a large degree, of young Australian and New Zealand backpackers and school groups. The interest and involvement displayed by young people in the Anzac Day celebrations is fascinating and gives a true indication of the campaign's place in Australia's history, national pride and self-perception.

In my youth, the conventional wisdom of the day was that Anzac would be forgotten as the veterans passed away. Despite the usual primary school lessons every April, as a young man I had little interest in the Gallipoli legend. My grandfathers fought at the Somme and in the Balkans as members of the British army, not at Gallipoli. Also, like many of my generation, I was busy in my youth protesting our involvement in the war in Vietnam.

It was only much later, after many years of researching, analysing and writing about the Australian character, that I became fascinated by the role of Anzac in our folklore. And for someone with no personal or family connection to the event itself, I was rather surprised to find that my September 2004 visit to the battlefields of Gallipoli was a deeply moving and emotional experience.

My idea had been to visit the area as research and background for this book. My main interest was to gain an understanding of the terrain and the landmarks that had become so familiar as I had collected and read and edited stories written about the campaign and its effects on the lives of Australians ninety years ago. My motivation for putting together this collection came from a more literary and sociological viewpoint than from any personal, military or historical perspective.

It wasn't until I stood at Ari Burnu Point, where the first boats touched the shore, with the water lapping my shoes and uncontrolled tears running down my face, that I fully realised how much the Gallipoli experience is a part of the Australian psyche. I was rather glad the battlefields and beaches were virtually deserted when I was there.

I am sure many Turks feel the same about the 'Battle of Canakkale'. Former New South Wales RSL president Rusty Priest once said, 'Australia and Turkey are perhaps the only two countries in the world that have a strong friendship born out of a war.' He meant, of course, a war in which the two countries were enemies.

***

A few days before reaching Anzac Cove, we sat having lunch on the deck of a wonderful seafood restaurant in the town of Gelibulou. This town is the 'Gallipoli' after which the peninsula is named. It is situated well north of the battlefields and was untouched by the battles which bear its name.

The blue waters of the Dardanelles sparkled all around us in the September sunshine as Ali and I spoke of our differing perceptions of the events of 1915. We agreed to disagree on several points and Ali concluded by stating that, to his way of thinking, the Gallipoli campaign changed the history of many nations, but affected three in particular.

'It helped make the nation of Turkey and it gave your new nation an identity,' he said. Then he added, 'And if we had lost and you had won, supplies and arms would have reached Russia and there would probably have been no Russian Revolution. Imagine how *that* would have changed world history.'

Ali could well be right. It is certainly food for thought.

Ali also claimed the Turks probably knew about the withdrawal from Anzac Cove and Suvla Bay, but let our troops go without further casualties because they were leaving. I think he is wrong on this point, of course. There is solid evidence that the Ottoman and German generals had no idea about the evacuation. It was one time when we actually got the better of the Turks at Gallipoli.

I can forgive Ali for this lapse. It would be impolite to argue every point with such a wonderful host. Ali is all that any visitor to Turkey could wish for as a guide and travelling companion.

***

Back here in Sydney, when I check the international football results online, I find myself hoping that Besiktas has won on the weekend . . . and Fenebache has lost.

Back in Istanbul, Ali Salih Dirik, long-distance supporter of the Sydney Swans, hopes that any other team has beaten Collingwood, and the Sydney Swans have been victorious in his nation's colours.

DUR YOLCU

NECMETTIN HALIL ONAN

Necmettin Halil Onan was born in 1902 in Çatalca, a rural district in Eastern Thrace on the European side of the Bosphorus, outside of Istanbul. He studied Turkish literature at Istanbul University and went to Ankara to join the national struggle during the civil war that followed WWI. After working for the Anatolian News Agency and in private schools, he was appointed Professor of Old Turkish Literature at Ankara University in 1942. He died in 1968. His two volumes of poetry were published in 1927 and 1933.

The first verse of this poem is carved into the hillside opposite Canakkale—it applies to all who fought at Gallipoli.

Dur yolcu, bilmeden gelip bastığın,
Bu toprak, bir devrin battığı yerdir.
Eğil de kulak ver, bu sessiz yığın,
Bir vatan kalbinin attığı yerdir!

Bu ıssız, gölgesiz yolun sonunda,
Gördüğün bu tümsek Anadolu'nda
İstiklal uğrunda, namus yolunda,
Can veren Mehmed'in yattığı yerdir!

Bu tümsek, koparken büyük zelzele,
Son vatan parçası geçerken ele,
Mehmed'in düşmanı boğduğu sele,
Mübarek kanını kattığı yerdir! . . .

Düşün ki haşrolan kan, kemik, etin
Yaptığı bu tümsek, amansız, çetin,
Bir harbin sonunda bütün milletin,
Hürriyet zevkini tattığı yerdir!

TRAVELLER, HALT (DUR YOLCU)

TRANSLATED TO ENGLISH RHYME
BY JIM HAYNES

Traveller, halt on this quiet mound.
This soil you thus tread, unaware,
Is where a generation ended . . . Listen,
The heart of a nation is beating there.

Where Anatolia meets the sea,
Here, at the end of our land,
For the sake of our independence,
Our soldiers made their stand.

From this mound arose our nation,
From this sacred sand and mud.
Our sons overwhelmed the invaders,
And bought freedom with their blood!

Think of the blood, bone and flesh
That made this sacred ground
When we fought in the war of all nations . . .
And halt, on this quiet mound.

TURKEY–AN ABBREVIATED HISTORY

JIM HAYNES

The nation of Turkey as we know it today did not exist in 1915. The Anzacs, and the other Allied forces on the Gallipoli Peninsula, were fighting against an army assembled by the Central Powers and consisting mostly of units of the Ottoman army, with some German officers and some German artillery. Although Turks made up a large part of the Ottoman army, its troops were actually an ethnic mixture that reflected the extent of the Ottoman Empire.

The people known as 'Turks' or 'Seljuks' or 'Seljuk Turks' were Muslims from central Asia, east of the Caspian Sea. They invaded Anatolia in 1071 and defeated the Christian Byzantine army at the battle of Manzikert. From that time onwards, the Christian religion and Greek language were gradually replaced in Anatolia by Islam and the Turkish language.

Christians in Western Europe sent a series of military expeditions called the Crusades to drive the Seljuk Turks from the Holy Land. However, the Seljuk Empire endured until 1243, when the Asian nomads known as Mongols invaded it.

The Mongol Empire was torn by internal struggles and soon fell apart. As a result, the Turks' influence in Anatolia grew. During the 1300s, a group of Turks who became known as the Ottomans began to build a mighty empire.

By the late 1300s, the Ottomans had conquered the western two-thirds of Anatolia, most of Thrace and much of the Balkan Peninsula, including Greece. In 1453, Ottoman forces led by Mehmet II captured Constantinople, ending the Byzantine

Empire. The Ottomans called the city Istanbul and made it their capital. After Ottoman forces conquered Syria in 1516 and Egypt in 1517, the empire became the leading naval power in the Mediterranean region.

By 1566, under Sultan Suleyman I (known as Suleyman the Magnificent), the Ottoman Empire extended from Hungary in Europe to Yemen in the south, Morocco in the west and Persia in the east. Five years later, in 1571, a European fleet defeated the Ottoman navy in the Battle of Lepanto, near Greece. The Ottoman Empire was in steady decline from that point until 1918.

In 1774, the Ottomans lost a six-year war against Russia and were forced to allow Russian ships to pass through the Dardanelles, the waters linking the Black Sea with the Mediterranean. The Ottoman Empire then lost the Crimea, a peninsula in the Black Sea, to Russia in 1783.

The empire also lost more territory during the 1800s. The Treaty of Adrianople acknowledged the independence of Greece and gave Russia control of the mouth of the Danube River. The Ottomans then conceded other Balkan territory in a series of wars with Russia, and lost Algeria and Tunisia to France and Cyprus to Britain.

During the late 1890s, small groups of students and military officers who opposed the empire's old, harsh policies banded together secretly. They were known as the Young Turks and the most influential group was the Committee of Union and Progress. In 1908, members of this group led a revolt against Sultan Abdulhamit and then ruled the empire using his brother, Mehmet V, as a puppet sultan.

Some Young Turks, such as Enver Pasha, wanted to restore the greatness of the Ottoman Empire. Others, like Mustafa Kemal, no longer cared about the idea of maintaining an empire and wished to establish a new Turkish nation.

And so the Ottoman Empire continued to crumble. Soon after the revolution in 1908, Bulgaria declared its independence, and Austria–Hungary annexed Bosnia–Herzegovina. Italy took Libya in 1912. In 1913, the Ottoman Empire surrendered Crete, part of

Macedonia, southern Epirus, and many Aegean islands to Greece. By 1914, the empire had lost all its European territory except eastern Thrace.

Enver Pasha, leader of the governing committee, had strong links with Germany and, in 1914, the Ottoman Empire entered World War I on the side of Germany and Austria–Hungary in an attempt to regain lost territory.

Many nationalists saw this as a bad move. Mustafa Kemal was of the opinion that it was a 'no win' situation for Turkey. If the Central Powers won, Turkey would be a satellite of Germany. If the Central Powers lost, Turkey lost everything.

In 1915, the British, French and Russians, with support from Greece, tried to gain control of the Straits so that aid could be shipped to Russia.

The Ottomans, with German help, defeated the British and French navies' attempt to force a passage through the Dardanelles in March 1915 and then successfully held the Gallipoli Peninsula, dealing the Allies a crushing defeat in their attempt to invade, which lasted from April to December 1915.

The Allies, however, won the war in 1918.

***

After World War I, the Allies set out to break up the Ottoman Empire. Allied troops occupied Istanbul and the Straits. In May 1919, Greek troops, protected by Allied fleets, landed at the Ottoman port of Izmir and advanced into the country. The Turks deeply resented the Ottoman government's inability to defend their homeland.

In August 1920, the sultan's government signed the harsh Treaty of Sevres with the Allies. The treaty granted independence to some parts of the empire and gave other parts to various Allied powers. The empire was reduced to Istanbul and a portion of Anatolia. As a result of the treaty, the sultan's popularity among the Turks declined further, while the power of the nationalists grew.

Mustafa Kemal was a Turkish military hero as a result of his bravery and leadership during the Gallipoli campaign. He quickly organised a nationalist movement. Under his leadership, a series of nationalist congresses met in Anatolian cities and formed a provisional government. In April 1920, a new Turkish Grand National Assembly met in Ankara and elected Kemal as its president.

In September 1922, the nationalist forces finally drove the Greeks from Turkey. The Allies agreed to draw up a new peace treaty with the nationalists. The Treaty of Lausanne, signed in 1923, set Turkey's borders about where they are today.

The Grand National Assembly proclaimed Turkey to be a republic on 29 October 1923 and elected Kemal as president. Kemal and other nationalist leaders believed that the new nation could not survive without sweeping social changes.

During the 1920s and 1930s, the government did away with traditions such as Muslim schools, the Islamic legal system, and the wearing of the veil by women and the fez by men. It abolished the religious and civil office of the caliph. Polygamy was outlawed and women received the right to vote and to hold public office.

One of the reforms to Europeanise Turkey was that all Turks were required to choose a family name. At the same time, the Grand National Assembly gave Kemal his surname, Ataturk, meaning 'Father of the Turks'.

***

Mustafa Kemal was born on 12 March 1881, in Thessaloniki, Greece (then part of the Ottoman Empire). He attended military schools and rose to the rank of general during World War I. He became famous for his role in defeating the Allies at Gallipoli Peninsula.

Kemal had originally been active as a young Turk but he disagreed with Enver and others on such issues as maintaining the empire and, later, joining the Germans in the war against

Britain, France and Russia. As a result he was never part of the ruling group and was sent as military attaché to Bulgaria in a form of exile.

It is ironic that the man who defeated us at Gallipoli was opposed to being involved in the war on the side of the Central Powers.

It can be argued that Kemal was the one man who stood between Allied victory and defeat at Gallipoli. It was he who anticipated the Allied moves and read the situation and reacted fastest on 25 April. It was he who ordered the 57th Regiment (significantly an all-Turkish regiment of the Ottoman army) to die in order to halt the Anzac advance. It was he who drove the New Zealanders and British from Chunuk Bair on 10 August and thus finally rendered the Allied August offensive futile.

Victory at Gallipoli was what gave Ataturk the kudos, credibility, popularity and power base to later lead the Turks to independence and create the nation we know today as Turkey. There is a certain irony in the fact that Kemal's own birthplace, Salonika, in Macedonia, part of the old Ottoman Empire, was not included in the Turkey he helped create; it is now part of Greece.

***

Ataturk served as Turkey's president until he died in 1938. His memory is still revered today and his photograph hangs in all public buildings.

Upon the death of Ataturk, Ismet Inonu became president and kept Turkey virtually neutral during World War II by avoiding entering the conflict until February 1945.

Turkey struggled to come to terms with its new identity as a democratic republic through the twentieth century. By the late 1950s, a rise in the national debt and restrictions on freedom of speech made the ruling Democrat Party unpopular and, in 1960, army units seized control of the government. Prime Minister Menderes was hanged for crimes against the nation and President Bayar was sentenced to life imprisonment but later released.

In 1961, Turkey adopted a new constitution and the provisional government then held open national elections. No party won a majority in the legislature. In the late 1960s, radical groups of Turks began staging bombings, kidnappings and murders in an attempt to overthrow the government.

In the 1970s, deep divisions developed between secular and religious groups. No political party could form a stable government. In 1980, the military again seized control of the government and remained in power until Turkey returned to civilian rule in 1983.

The Motherland Party controlled the government from 1983 until the True Path Party won the most legislative seats in the 1991 elections and Tansu Ciller became Turkey's first female prime minister.

In the elections held in 1995, the Welfare Party, a strongly pro-Islamic party, won the most seats in the legislature but, in 1998, the Constitutional Court banned the Welfare Party, ruling that its goal of creating an Islamic state was unconstitutional.

This type of instability has been the norm in Turkey over the past seventy years, with political parties forming, merging and re-forming constantly.

Turkey has also been beset by other problems. Since the 1960s there has been unrest in Cyprus, which remains politically divided. The government has battled Kurdish guerrillas in south-eastern Turkey and, since the 1980s, 30,000 people have died in the fighting. In August 1999, a powerful earthquake struck north-western Turkey, killing more than 17,000 people. Then, in 2001, the national currency lost about half its value, thousands of businesses closed, and hundreds of thousands of workers lost their jobs.

The European Union accepted Turkey as a candidate for membership in 1999, but political and economic reforms are required before the EU will set a timetable for membership. In 2002 Turkey abolished the use of capital punishment during peacetime and expanded civil rights.

Turkey is a nation torn between old traditional values and the modern world. It is both European and Middle Eastern, sectarian and Muslim. The long process of evolution into a successful and independent nation, begun by Kemal Ataturk, is not yet complete, but Turkey is a proud country with a unique heritage and at least her future is now in her own hands.

BIBLIOGRAPHY

Askin, M. *Gallipoli: A Turning Point*, Mustafa Askin, Canakkale, Turkey, 2002.

Baylebridge, W. *An Anzac Muster*, Angus & Robertson, 1962 (first published in 1921).

Bean, C.E.W. (ed.) *The Anzac Book*, Cassell, London, 1916.

Bean, C.E.W. *The Story of Anzac*, Vol II, Angus & Robertson, Sydney, 1935.

Beeston, J.L. *Five Months at Anzac*, Angus & Robertson, Sydney, 1916.

Birdwood, W. *Khaki and Gown: An Autobiography*, Ward Lock, London, 1941.

Bridges, R. *The Immortal Dawn*, Hodder & Stoughton, London, 1917.

Buley, E.C. *Glorious Deeds of Australasians in the Great War*, Andrew Melrose, London, 1915.

Carlyon, L. *Gallipoli*, Pan MacMillan, Sydney, 2001.

Cavill, H.W. *Imperishable Anzacs: A Story of Australia's Famous First Brigade from the Diary of Pte. Harold Walter Cavill No. 27 1 Bn.*, William Brooks & Co, Sydney, 1916.

Coulthard-Clark, C. *The Encyclopedia of Australian Battles*, Allen & Unwin, Sydney, 1998.

Dinning, H. *By-ways on Service: Notes from an Australian Journal*, Constable, London, 1918.

Fahey, W. *Diggers' Songs*, AMHP, Sydney, 1966.

Fewster, K., Basarm, V. and Vasarm, H. *Gallipoli: The Turkish Story*, Allen & Unwin, Sydney, 1985/2003.

Hanman, E.F. *Twelve Months with the 'Anzacs'*, Watson, Ferguson & Co., Brisbane, 1916.

Hogue, O. *Love Letters of an Anzac*, Melrose, London, 1916.

——*Trooper Bluegum at the Dardanelles*, Melrose, London, 1916.

Kent, D. *From Trench and Troopship*, Hale & Iremonger, Sydney, 1999.

Kent, D. (ed.) *Kia Ora Coo-ee: The Magazine for the ANZACS in the Middle East*, 1918, Cornstalk/Angus & Robertson, Sydney, 1981.

Kinross, P. *Ataturk: The Rebirth of a Nation*, Weidenfeld/Phoenix, London, 1991/1993.

Livesey, A. *Great Battles of World War I*, Guild, London, 1989.

Loch, F.S. *The Straits Impregnable*, John Murray, London, 1917.

Perry, R. *Monash: The Outsider Who Won a War*, Random House, Sydney, 2004.

Phillips, W. *Australians in World War One: Gallipoli*, Phillips, Coffs Harbour, 2001.

Pope, E. and Wheal, E. *Dictionary of the First World War*, MacMillan, London, 1995.

Pugsley, C. *The Anzacs at Gallipoli*, Lothian, Melbourne, 2000.

Rudd, S. *Memoirs of Corporal Keeley*, University of Queensland Press, Brisbane, 1971 (first published in 1918).

Skeyhill, T. *A Singing Soldier*, Knickerbocker Press, New York, 1919.

——*Soldier Songs from Anzac*, George Robertson & Co., Melbourne, 1915.

Steel, N. and Hart, P. *Defeat at Gallipoli*, MacMillan, London, 1994.

Travers, T. *Gallipoli 1915*, Tempus Publishing, Stroud, UK, 2001/2004.

Uluarslan, H. *Gallipoli Campaign*, Zeki & Uluarslan, Canakkale, Turkey, 2001.

Various, *An Anzac Memorial*, Returned Sailors and Soldiers League, Sydney, 1919.

ACKNOWLEDGEMENTS

THANKS TO:

The Australian War Memorial
The Mitchell Library, State Library of New South Wales
The Turkish Embassy, Canberra
The late Alan Murphy
Rebecca Kaiser
Michelle Swainson
Susin Chow
Jo Lyons
Julia Eim
Stuart Neal
Robyn McMillan

Turkey
Ali Salih Dirik
Our driver, Mehemet
NUR Travel Istanbul